POCSO COMPASS: NURTURING SAFE CHILDHOODS AND SHIELDING INNOCENCE

An In-Depth Guide for Legal Professionals, Activists, Educators, and Parents in India

NAVIN KUMAR AGARWAL

ISBN 000-0-00000-000-0

"The purity and innocence of a child are not only the foundation of their humanity but also the hope for a better and more compassionate world. To protect their innocence is to preserve the essence of our collective humanity."

– Unknown

Contents

Preface

Child sexual abuse is a pervasive problem that affects millions of children worldwide. In India, the Protection of Children from Sexual Offences (POCSO) Act, 2012, is a vital legal instrument that aims to safeguard children from sexual exploitation and abuse. The Act defines a child as any person under the age of eighteen years and covers various forms of sexual abuse, including sexual harassment, assault, and exploitation.

The book starts with an introduction to the issue of child sexual abuse and the need for a robust legal framework to combat it. It goes on to provide a detailed analysis of the POCSO Act, highlighting key provisions, such as the definition of sexual offences against children, the punishment for offenders, the role of law enforcement agencies, and the procedures for reporting and investigating cases of abuse. It is intended for a wide range of readers, including, lawyers, law enforcement officers, child rights activists, social workers, teachers, parents, and anyone else who is concerned about child protection and welfare. This book also provides basic guidelines as to how they can educate children about the sexual threats through games and activities.

Moreover, the book also examines the various challenges in implementing the Act, such as the low conviction rates, the lack of awareness among stakeholders, and the need for better victim support services.

Overall, this book is a timely and vital resource for anyone concerned about protecting children from sexual abuse and exploitation. It provides a comprehensive understanding of the POCSO Act and the challenges faced in implementing it, while offering practical solutions for improving the legal and social response to child sexual abuse in India. With its insightful analysis and recommendations, this book serves as an essential guide for anyone interested in the well-being and protection of children.

CHAPTER

01

Understanding POCSO: An Introduction

Why was the POCSO Act enacted?

The POCSO Act was enacted to protect children from offences of sexual assault, sexual harassment and pornography and to provide a child-friendly system for the trial of these offences. There has been an increase in sexual offences against children. The increasing incidence of sexual offences against children had to be addressed through a separate law, as the Indian Penal Code (IPC) did not specifically provide for sexual offences against children, particularly boys. It recognized limited forms of sexual violence against girls, and actions other than rape were regarded as "offending the modesty of women", punishable with a maximum of two years and / or fine. Controversially worded Section 377, IPC, which criminalized the voluntary act of intercourse against the order of nature, was the only provision available to address penetrative sexual assault against boys.

The need to protect the interest of the child victim and the child witness was also recognized. Since regular criminal court procedures and processes are not suited to a child. POCSO Act provides for child-friendly measures and procedures at every stage of the legal process. It requires special treatment of cases related to child sexual abuse such as the establishment of special courts, special prosecutors and persons assisting child victims. The recording of the complaint, recording of evidence, investigation and trial of offences should be done in a child friendly manner and the dignity and autonomy of the child must be respected. The enactment is in consonance of various provision specified in the Constitution of India.

When did the POCSO Act come into force?

The POCSO Act received the assent of the President on 19 June 2012 and came into force on 14 November 2012, through a Gazette notification dated 9 November 2012.

Is the POCSO Act applicable across India?

The Act applies to the whole of India including the Jammu and Kashmir with effect from 31st August 2019.

What are the sexual offences which are recognized under the POCSO Act?

The POCSO Act recognizes seven types of sexual offences. They are:

- penetrative sexual assault,
- aggravated penetrative sexual assault,
- sexual assault,
- aggravated sexual assault,
- sexual harassment,
- use of a child for pornographic purposes, and
- storage of pornographic materials involving a child.

Abetment, or attempt to commit any of the above offences, are also considered as offences and are punishable under this Act.

What is the definition of 'child' under the POCSO Act?

Under the POCSO (Protection of Children from Sexual Offences) Act, 2012, a child is defined as any person below the age of 18 years. The act recognizes that children are vulnerable and need special protection against sexual offenses due to their age and immaturity. Therefore, the act provides for stringent punishments and special procedures to ensure the safety and privacy of child victims. It also recognizes the need to protect the interests of child witnesses and provides for child-friendly measures and procedures at every stage of the legal process.

Whether any specific gender is provided protection under the POCSO Act?

This Act is a gender equal and neutral Act, where any minor (irrespective of gender) will be taken care of. The Act recognizes that all children are vulnerable and need special protection against sexual offenses, irrespective of their gender.

Why was the Criminal Law (Amendment) Act, 2013 (the CLAA) enacted?

The Criminal Law Amendment Act, 2013 was enacted in response to the Delhi gang rape incident commonly known as "Nirbhaya Case", which highlighted the shortcomings of the existing law in addressing sexual offences.

The Criminal Law Amendment Act 2013 was passed by Parliament on April 2, 2013, based on the recommendation of the Verma Committee. The Amendment Act introduces several important and procedural changes to the three main criminal law statutes: The Indian Penal Code, 1860 (IPC); The Code of Criminal Procedure, 1973 (The CRPC), and the Indian Evidence Act, 1872 (The Evidence Act).

The POCSO Act not only introduces new categories of crimes against women, but also clarifies the procedure to be followed for investigation, medical examination, trial and appreciation of evidence in relation to these crimes. Prior to the CLAA, the IPC recognized a very limited range of sexual offences, which were defined very narrowly.

The only recognised offences in this category were:

a) Outraging the modesty of a woman (section 354)
b) Kidnapping a woman to compel her marriage (section 366)
c) Selling a minor for purposes of prostitution (section 372)
d) Rape
e) Unnatural sexual offence (section 377)
f) Intercourse during separation (section 376A)
g) Custodial Rape (Section 376B, Section 376C and section 376D)
h) Word, gesture or Act intended to outrage the modesty of a women (Section 509)

The CLAA corrects this inadequacy by adding several new offences and redefining old offences. In addition, the new law has significantly increased the punishment under existing crimes against women and has prescribed higher minimum mandatory sentences to be given to them. The CLAA also allows the victim to collect fines collected under these offences.

What are the key amendments introduced by the Criminal Law (Amendment) Act, 2013?

The CLAA introduced several new offences and redefined the offence of rape and trafficking in the IPC.

New offences introduced:

a. Acid attacks (inserted as section 326A and section 326B, IPC)
b. Sexual harassment (inserted as section 354A, IPC)
c. Assault or use of criminal force to woman with intent to disrobe (inserted as section 354B, IPC)
d. Voyeurism (inserted as section 354C, IPC)
e. Stalking (inserted as section 354D, IPC)
f. Punishment for causing death or resulting in persistent vegetative state of victim (inserted as section 376A, IPC)
g. Sexual intercourse by a person in authority (inserted as section 376C, IPC)
h. Gang rape (inserted as section 376D, IPC)
i. Punishment for repeat offenders (inserted as section 376E, IPC). The Act makes certain repeat sexual offences punishable with a minimum mandatory period of 20 years or with death.

Except trafficking, the newly introduced sexual offences under the IPC will not be applicable where the victim is a minor boy.

Redefining of offences:

a. Rape (section 375 of the IPC amended via section 9 of the CLAA): The amendment provides a broader definition of 'rape' and is no longer limited to non-consensual penetrative penovaginal intercourse but includes all forms of penetrative assault.
b. Trafficking (section 370 of the IPC amended via section 8 of the CLAA): This amendment removes the obsolete provision covering 'buying or disposing of any person as a slave' and provides for detailed definition of the offence of trafficking. The provision also provides for more stringent sentencing with a mandatory sentence of life imprisonment which will mean imprisonment for the remainder of the person's natural life in certain serious cases.

c. Aggravated cases of rape (section 376(2) of the IPC amended by section 9 of the CLAA): The amendment has added additional offences under this category that attract more stringent punishment than the offence of rape.

Amendments to the CrPC:

a. Information given by a woman against whom any sexual offence under the IPC is allegedly committed or attempted must be recorded by a woman police officer or any woman officer. The recording of such information must be videographed and the police officer must get her statement recorded by a Judicial Magistrate as soon as possible. Further, if the woman is temporarily or permanently mentally or physically disabled, then such information must be recorded by a police officer, at her residence or at a convenient place of her choice, in the presence of an interpreter or special educator. [Proviso to section 154(1), CrPC]
b. Statement of a girl against whom any sexual offence under the IPC is allegedly committed or attempted must be recorded by a woman police officer or woman officer. [Proviso to section 161(2), CrPC]
c. The Judicial Magistrate must record the statement of a victim of any sexual offence as soon as the commission of the offence is brought to the notice of the police. [Section 164(5A), CrPC]
d. If the victim is temporarily or permanently mentally or physically disabled, the Magistrate must take the assistance of an interpreter or a special educator while recording her statement and such statement should be video graphed. Such statement will also be considered in lieu of examination in-chief, and the woman can be cross-examined on such statement without the need for recording it at the time of trial. [Proviso to section 164(5A)(a) and section 164(5A)(b), CrPC]
e. No sanction is required for prosecuting a public servant charged with any sexual offence under the IPC. [Explanation to section 192, CrPC]
f. The court must take appropriate measures to ensure that a victim of sexual offence is not confronted by the accused at the time of recording the evidence, while also ensuring the right of cross-examination of the accused. [Proviso to section 273, CrPC]
g. When the inquiry or trial relates to rape, causing injury in the course of rape which causes the death of a woman or causes her to be in a persistent

vegetative state, sexual intercourse by husband upon his wife during separation, sexual intercourse by a person in authority or gang rape, the trial must be completed within a period of two months from the date of filing the charge-sheet. [Proviso to section 309(1), CrPC]

h. All public or private hospitals, whether run by the Central/ State Government, local bodies or any other persons are under an obligation to provide immediate, first-aid or medical treatment to victims of sexual offences free of cost. [Section 357 C, CrPC]

i. Where the person identifying the arrested person is mentally or physically disabled, the identification process should be supervised by a Judicial Magistrate and video graphed. [Proviso to section 54(A), CrPC].

Amendments to the Evidence Act:

a. Introduction of 'section 53A' to the Evidence Act whereby it makes previous sexual experience irrelevant to determining consent in respect of sexual offences.

b. Amendment to section 114A by which a court may presume the absence of consent in all cases of aggravated rape falling under section 376(2).

c. Amendment to the proviso under section 146 whereby the questioning of a victim of sexual offences in a manner that calls into question the general immoral character or the previous sexual experience is now prohibited.

Do the POCSO Act and the Criminal Law (Amendment) Act contain any special measures for children with disabilities?

Yes, both the Acts have the following provisions for children with disabilities:

a) Offences: Under the POCSO Act, if a person takes advantage of the mental or physical disability of a child to commit penetrative sexual assault, it would be aggravated offence and is punishable with fine and a minimum term of rigorous imprisonment of 10 years that may extend to life imprisonment. It also forms a basis for aggravated non-penetrating sexual assault, which is punishable with fine and a minimum sentence of 5 years imprisonment and a maximum sentence of 7 years. Similarly, assault (penetrating or non-penetrating) resulting in physical disability, mental illness, or any type of temporary or permanent impairment is also an aggravated offence.

b) The commission of rape on a girl suffering from mental or physical disability is a ground for aggravated rape under the amended IPC and will now be punished with fine and rigorous imprisonment for a minimum term of ten years which may extend to life imprisonment. In addition, rape that causes death or causes the girl to remain in a vegetative state is sentenced to a minimum of 20 years of rigorous imprisonment, which may extend to life imprisonment.

c) Recording of information: As per the amendment of CRPC by CLAA, the information given by a girl, against whom sexual offence have allegedly been committed or attempted, should be recorded by a female police officer or a female officer. In addition, if the girl is temporarily or permanently physically or mentally disabled, information must be recorded at her place of residence or at her place of choice, in the presence of an interpreter or special educator and must be video graphed.

d) Identification of the arrested person: A Judicial Magistrate must monitor the identification of an arrested person by a mentally or physically disabled child and ensure that the manner in which the child is comfortable is used. The process will also have to be video graphed.

e) Recording of statements: Under the POCSO Act, while recording the statement of a child victim suffering from a physical or mental disability, the police or magistrate may enlist the assistance of a special educator, qualified expert, or any person who is familiar with the manner of communication of the child. The state government will have to pay for this service.

f) The magistrate should seek the assistance of an interpreter or special educator while recording the statement of a girl who is temporarily or permanently mentally or physically handicapped. Such statement should also be video graphed. Further, such statement shall be deemed to be in place of the examination-in-chief and the girl can be cross-examined on it. The statement should not be recorded afresh at the time of trial.

g) Evidence: The Special Court can enlist the help of a special educator, qualified expert or anyone who is familiar with the way the child communicates while recording the child's evidence. A witness who is unable to speak can give his evidence in any other intelligible manner, as by writing or by signs. Such writings or signs must be made in the open court and shall be considered oral evidence. If the witness is unable to communicate verbally, the court should enlist the help of an interpreter or a special educator and also videograph the statement.

h) Compensation: While ordering compensation, the Special Court can consider whether the child has acquired disability as a result of the crime committed against him/ her.

In the event that provisions of another Act are inconsistent with the POCSO Act, which Act will override?

Being a special law, the POCSO Act will govern the field on sexual offences against children. Further, Section 42A of the Act expressly states that in the event of inconsistency between this Act and any other law, the POCSO Act shall override. For example, under IPC, sexual intercourse by a man with his wife who is more than 15 years of age is not rape. No such exception has been provided under the POCSO Act. Therefore, this is an inconsistency between the POCSO Act and the IPC. Due to its overriding effect, a person who has intercourse with his wife who is between the ages of 15 and 18 years can be prosecuted under the POCSO Act.

In what way is the procedure under the POCSO Act different from regular criminal procedure?

The procedure prescribed under the POCSO Act is much more child-accessible and friendly than the procedure laid down in the Criminal Procedure Code (CrPC). There has also been an attempt to incorporate the guidelines laid down by the Supreme Court in Sakshi v. Union of India, AIR 2004 SC 3566 Act. The main procedural differences are listed below:

a. ***Location for recording the statement:*** Under the POCSO Act, the statement of a child under 18 years of age must be recorded at the place of the child's choice. This may be the place in which the child normally resides or any other place of child's choice. Under CrPC, the statement of a person under 15, regardless of gender, and the woman should be taken in the place in which they reside and not in the police station. As is clear, the POCSO Act provides an option for the child, and it also requires that the statement of all persons under 18 years of age be recorded in this way.

b. ***Questions to be put to the child only by the Special Judge:*** Under the POCSO Act, the child cannot be questioned directly by the Special Public Prosecutor or the lawyer of the accused. Instead, all questions must be placed by the judge to the child. In a regular trial, the public prosecutor mainly conducts the examination in chief and the lawyer for the accused asks the questions in cross-examination. In Sakshi v. Union of India, the Supreme Court had directed that in cases of child sexual abuse or rape, the question should be given in writing to the Presiding Officer of the court during the cross-examination on behalf of the accused, who could then put it to the child in a clear language which is not embarrassing to the child. The POCSO Act goes one step further and requires all questions by the Special Public Prosecutor to be put to the child by the Special Judge.

c. ***Presumption of culpable mental state:*** Under the POCSO Act, if a person is prosecuted for allegedly committing, abetting, or attempting to commit penetrative sexual assault, aggravated penetrative sexual assault, sexual assault, or aggravated sexual assault, then the court will assume that the person has actually committed a crime, abetted, or attempted to commit a crime. The onus is on the accused to establish his/her innocence. This is a marked departure from normal criminal procedure and evidence under which the burden is on the prosecution to establish the offence beyond all reasonable doubt.

d. ***Direct cognizance by the Special Court:*** Under the CRPC, the Magistrate will have to take cognizance of any criminal case and transfer the case to the respective courts on the basis of jurisdiction. Cases cannot lie directly before the Sessions Court. For example, in a rape case, the police will report to the Magistrate and since the Magistrate's Court does not have jurisdiction over rape cases, it will be transferred to the Sessions Court when the preliminary process is completed. Under the POCSO Act, however, the Special Court can take cognizance of the offences directly and will not have to wait for the Magistrate's Court to commit the matter in this case.

Who are the key authorities under the POCSO Act and what are their duties towards child victims of sexual offences?

The key authorities and their duties are as follows:

Key Authorities under the POCSO Act and their duties	
Authority under the POCSO Act d Central Rules	**Duties**
Child Welfare Committee	• Determining a suitable placement for a child who has been abused or is facing a threat of abuse in her/his place of residence, within three days. • Providing a support person to a child for assistance during the investigation and trial with the consent of the child and her/his parent, guardian, or person whom the child trusts.
District Child Protection Unit (DCPU)	• Maintaining a register with names, addresses and contact details of interpreters, translators, and special educators. • Making the register available to the SJPU, local police, magistrate, or Special Court. • Making payments for services to the above experts, from funds at their disposal.
Police/Special Juvenile Police Unit[1] (SJPU)	• Recording information pertaining to the commission of an offence, or apprehension that it is likely to be committed. • Making a preliminary assessment as to whether the child is in need of care and protection and if so, taking immediate steps to ensure protection. • Reporting the case to the Special Court and the Child Welfare Committee (CWC) within 24 hours of receiving the report about the commission of the crime. • Producing the child before the CWC within 24 hours if the child has been abused or faces the risk of further abuse in the place where the child is residing, or if the child is without parental support. • Taking the child for medical examination to a medical practitioner in a government hospital or to a private hospital in the event that a registered medical practitioner is not available at the government hospital. • Ensuring that if required, the child receives emergency medical care at the nearest hospital. • Recording the statement of the child at a place of his or her choice. • Ensuring that the child is not exposed to the accused during investigation. • Providing information about the procedures, developments in the case, and services to the child, parent/ guardian, support person, etc. • Ensuring that the statement of the child is recorded by the nearest lady Magistrate, and within 24 hours.

1. Under Section 63 of the Juvenile Justice (Care and Protection of Children) Act, 2000, Special Juvenile Police Units (SJPUs) may be created by State Governments in every district and city to co-ordinate and upgrade the police treatment of juveniles and children.

Key Authorities under the POCSO Act and their duties	
Magistrate	• Recording the statement of the child in a child friendly manner and by audio-video electronic means, with the assistance of experts, special educators, translators, or interpreters, if necessary. • Recording such statement within 24 hours of the police receiving information about the alleged commission of a sexual offence.
Special Court and Judge	• Conducting in camera trials of offences under the POCSO Act. • Ensuring that a child-friendly atmosphere is maintained in the Court and that the dignity, interests, and identity of the child are respected and protected during trial. • Recording the evidence of the child within 30 days and completing the trial within 1 year of taking up the matter, as far as possible. • Ordering payment of compensation in appropriate cases.
Special Public Prosecutor	• Prosecution of cases exclusively under the POCSO Act.
Support Person	• Maintaining confidentiality of all information pertaining to the child, to which she/he has access. • Keeping the child, parent/guardian, or other person in whom the child has trust and confidence informed about the proceedings in the case, including available assistance, judicial procedures, and potential outcomes. • Informing the child of the role she/he may play in the judicial process. • Ensuring that any concerns the child may have, regarding safety in relation to the accused and the manner in which testimony is provided, are conveyed to the relevant authorities.
Central Government	• Giving wide publicity to the provisions of the POCSO Act at regular intervals through the media including television, radio and print media. • Imparting periodic training to government officers, police, and others on matters related to the implementation of the Act. • Framing Rules to give effect to the provisions of the Act. • Passing orders to remove difficulties that may arise in giving effect to the provisions of the Act, within two years from the commencement of the Act, i.e., 13 November 2014.

Key Authorities under the POCSO Act and their duties	
State Government	• Designating a Court of Sessions to be a Special Court under this Act in every district. • Appointing a Special Public Prosecutor for every such Special Court. • Promoting wide publicity of the provisions of the Act through media at regular intervals to spread awareness among the public, particularly children, their parents and guardians. • Training police and other officers of the State Government on matters relating to the implementation of the provisions of the Act. • Framing guidelines for use by all persons who are to be associated with the pretrial and trial stage to assist the child. These include NGOs, professionals and experts or persons having knowledge of psychology, social work, physical health, mental health and child development. • Paying compensation from the Victims Compensation Fund or other schemes for the purpose of compensation and rehabilitating victims, within 30 days from the order of the Special Court.
National Commission for Protection of Child Rights and State Commissions for Protection of Child Rights	• Monitoring the implementation of the POCSO Act by the Central and State Governments. • Calling for reports from the CWC on specific cases. • Reporting on the implementation of the Act by way of a separate chapter in its Annual Report.

CHAPTER

Jurisdiction 02

Which court has been assigned the responsibility of adjudicating cases related to violations of the POCSO Act?

A Special Court under the POCSO Act is a Sessions Court designated in each district to be a Special Court by the State Government for trying offences under the Act. The State Government should notify such Special Courts in consultation with the Chief Justice. The Special Court have been provided to ensure speedy trial of sexual offences against children under the POCSO Act. All offences under the POCSO Act will be tried by a Special Court. In the event that a Children's Court has been notified for the Protection of Children's Rights Act, 2005, or any other Special Court has already been designated for similar purposes under any other law; such court shall be considered as Special Court for the purpose of the POCSO Act. The Special Court, however, cannot try offences committed by a juvenile i.e., a person under 18 years of age. This case will lie before the Juvenile Justice Board constituted under the Juvenile Justice (Care and Protection of Children) Act, 2000 in such cases.

Generally, the term 'Special Court' denotes that it is a court designated only for the hearing of cases under the act under which it is established. Therefore, the Special Court under the POCSO Act will only hear cases under the POCSO Act. However, it is possible that an act constitutes an offence under the POCSO Act as well as the Indian Penal Code or any other law, and an accused is charged under more than one law.

For example, if a child has been sexually as well as physically abused, the act will be a sexual offence under the POCSO Act and will also constitute an offence under the Indian Penal Code. In such cases, the Special Court may conduct a trial for both sets of offences, even if the offence of hurt is not awarded under the POCSO Act. In such cases, the Special Court should prescribe a sentence under the law which provides for maximum punishment. For example, where a girl under the age of 16 is raped, POCSO sets a minimum sentence of seven years under the offence of 'penetrative sexual assault' which can carry up to life imprisonment. But the same crime constitutes aggravated rape under Section 376 (2) (i) of the IPC and under this law - the greater degree of punishment is prescribed i.e., the minimum sentence of ten years which may extend to life imprisonment. Therefore, the Special Court should implement the IPC sentence as it is greater.

The Special Court may also try offences under Section 67B of the Information Technology Act, 2000 which relate to the publication or transmission of sexually explicit material depicting children or facilitating the abuse of children online. A Children's Court which acts as a Special Court under the POCSO Act, however, may also try offences other than sexual offences against children.

A Magistrate cannot try offences under the POCSO Act. The power to try offences under the POCSO Act is vested only with a Special Court. The role of a magistrate is very limited - they can only record the victim's statement under section 164 of the CrPC. The magistrate can record the victim's statements from any crime and not necessarily an offence under the POCSO Act.

The following offences mentioned under the POCSO Act can be heard by the Special Court:

- ***Sexual offences:*** Penetrative sexual assault, aggravated penetrative sexual assault, sexual assault, aggravated sexual assault, sexual harassment, use of a child for pornographic purposes, storage of pornographic materials involving a child are the seven types of sexual offences under this Act.
- ***Attempt/ Abetment:*** Any attempt to commit any of the above offences or any abetment i.e., assistance or help in committing the offence are also considered as offences and are punishable under this law.
- ***Media violation:*** If any person violates the privacy of child by giving details that could lead to the identification of the child, this amounts to an offence and is punishable by the Special Court.
- ***False Complaints:*** The Special Court can also take up the cases of incorrect or false complaints. For example, C wants to teach a lesson to his friend A, as C is jealous of A having a very close and friendly relationship with B. C files a complaint that A has sexually abused B. B had no complaint against A as he has not harmed her. A case of false complaint can be booked against C.

- ***Failure to report:*** Cases against people who have failed to file a complaint (mandatory reporting) despite being aware of the commission of the offence or aware that the offence may occur.
- ***Failure to record cases:*** The Special Court can also take up cases against the police who failed to record the cases when the complainant approaches them.
- ***Offences under other Acts:*** In situations where the Special Court is hearing an offence under this Act, the Special Court may also hear offences alleged to have been committed by the accused under some other law, provided that both/all the offences were committed in the same transaction.
- ***Offence under Section 67B of the Information Technology Act, 2000:*** The Special Court has the power to hear cases relating to publication or transmission of sexually explicit material depicting children any act or manner or which facilitates abuse of children.

The following procedures to be followed under the POCSO Act by the Special Court:

- The Special Court has the power to directly assume jurisdiction over a case without the need for it to be referred to the court by the Magistrate Court.
- Questions to the child must be put by the judge during the hearing on evidence.
- The child must be given frequent breaks during the recording of evidence.
- Video conferencing, curtains or one-way mirror can be used to prevent the child from seeing the accused while child's evidence is being recorded.
- The child must be questioned in a child friendly manner.
- The court must ensure that child is not called repeatedly to testify in court.
- The child's identity must be protected throughout the proceedings. The permission to disclose the identity of the child must be given only if it is in her/his best interest.
- The trial must be held *in camera*, which means that the general public must not be allowed in the Court.

All cases are to be prosecuted by a Special Public Prosecutor before a Special Court. A lawyer who has a minimum of 7 years of experience may be appointed by the State Government through a notification as a Special Public Prosecutor to prosecute all cases exclusively under this Act.

The Special Court can obtain cases under this Act directly from the complainant or on the basis of the police report. The court does not require a magistrate to refer/ transfer/ commit such cases to the Special Court.

All court proceedings under the POCSO Act are to be held in camera and are therefore not open to the public. The purpose of in-camera proceedings is to protect the privacy and dignity of the child victim and to prevent any further trauma or harm to the victim. Only persons related to the case are allowed inside the court room, i.e., both parties, the child's parents / family members / guardians and support persons (if appointed), the advocate for the accused and the Special Public Prosecutor.

In addition, the child is not required to be present for all proceedings. The child is to attend the proceedings only during the giving on his / her statements (if necessary) and hearing on evidence, if video conferencing is not conducted for proof of recording.

The Special Court may compensate the victim for any physical or mental trauma caused or immediate rehabilitation of the child. The Special Court has all the powers of the Sessions Court to try the offences mentioned under the POCSO Act and must conduct the proceedings in accordance with the Code of Criminal Procedure. The Special Court can award compensation under four grounds:

- When there is any loss or injury caused to the child. For instance, compensation may be granted if the child has suffered a fracture which occurred during the commission of the offence.
- For any physical or mental trauma that the child has undergone because of the offence.
- To meet the immediate needs of the child. For e.g., compensation may be granted to enable the child to avail of urgent medical intervention if s/he has suffered internal organ injuries.
- For rehabilitation of the child.

Exclusion: A child who commits an offence under the POCSO Act cannot be prosecuted before a Special Court. Such a child can only be dealt with by the Juvenile Justice Board (JJB) as per the procedure laid down under the

Juvenile Justice (Care and Protection of Children) Act, 2000. If a question arises about the age of the person produced before the particular court, it can determine such a question by satisfying itself about the age of the person and put its findings and reasons in writing. If the person is found to be a child, the case should be immediately transferred to the JJB, under whose jurisdiction it would lie.

CHAPTER

03

Reporting and Procedures

Police or the Special Juvenile Police Unit (SJPU) can be held liable for failure to follow child-friendly procedures under the POCSO Act. The penalty for such failure has been prescribed under IPC.

Under section 166A of the IPC, a public servant, who wilfully disobeys any direction of law, which requires the presence of him or any person at any place for the purpose of investigation in crime or any other matter can be punished with fine and rigorous imprisonment for a minimum term of six months which may extend to two years. For example, if a sub-inspector calls a child to a police station to record her statement or detains her in the police station at night, he can be held liable under IPC.

A public servant is also liable for the same punishment if he wilfully disobeys, to the prejudice of any person, any other direction of the law in the manner in which he should or should not investigate. For example, under Section 24 (3) of the POCSO Act, the investigating officer must ensure that the child is not in contact with the accused during the investigation. Failure to ensure this may result in criminal prosecution.

Similarly, the police or the SJPU can be held liable under the POCSO Act as well as the IPC for failure to record information about the alleged commission of offences under the POCSO Act and is punishable with imprisonment which may extend to six months and/or with fine. Under the IPC it is punishable for failure to record information about the alleged commission of sexual offences and has a minimum of six months of rigorous imprisonment that can extend to two years.

Is it Mandatory to report offences under the POCSO Act?

Yes. All persons are obliged to report offences under the POCSO Act. According to Section 19 (1), whoever knows that someone committed a crime or believes that he is likely to commit, should inform the Special Juvenile Police Unit (SJPU) or the local police. Failure to report an offence to the

Commission of offence is punishable under Section 21 (1) with a maximum of six months imprisonment and / or fine. The complaint can be filed by the victim, family member of the victim, an eyewitness or anyone who has received or has the information about either commission of such crime or an expectation that such crime is going to occur.

Children are also obliged to report offences under this Act. However, they cannot be punished for failure to report a crime.

The term 'mandatory reporting' does not appear in the POCSO Act. However, by setting a maximum sentence of six months imprisonment and / or a fine for failure to report in a sexual offence case, the Act makes it mandatory for people to report. It is important to note that failure to report an apprehension that a crime is likely to occur is not punishable. A child who fails to report the commission of a crime, makes a false complaint, or gives false information about the commission of a crime, cannot be held liable. Children are exempted from fines imposed under the Act for such offences.

There are two situations in which a person is expected to report an offence:

1) Where a sexual offence has already been committed against a child.
2) Where there is an apprehension that a sexual offence is likely to be committed against a child.

Thus, a person does not have to wait for the actual occurrence of the offence and can even report to the police or the SJPU if it is likely that a child may be abused.

The police and the SJPU are under an obligation to file complaints or information related to crimes under the Act. Where a crime has already been committed or attempted, a First Information Report (FIR) should be filed and registered, and a copy of the FIR handed over to the informer. If the police or SJPU refuse to register a crime or fail, they can face a maximum of six months imprisonment and/or a fine under the POCSO Act and a minimum of six months of rigorous imprisonment that may extend to two years under the IPC.

When the complainant is the victim in person(himself/herself) then it is of utmost importance that the police officer recording the statement makes the atmosphere friendly and suitable for the victim The help of a psychiatrist should preferably be taken as the incident would have shaken the victim inside-out. These steps would help the officer getting the accurate narration of the incident and details required for the case.

According to the proviso to Section 154(1) of the CrPC, if information is being given by a girl against whom any sexual offence under the IPC has been committed or attempted, it must be recorded by a woman police officer or any woman officer. This procedural rule will also apply to cases falling under the POCSO Act, an act as a sexual offence under the POCSO Act will also be a sex offence under the IPC. Therefore, if the first information about the crime is being given by a girl child - it must be filed by a female police officer or a female officer.

If a child is temporarily or permanently mentally or physically disabled and wishes to report a sexual offence that has been allegedly committed or attempted against her, then the police must record such information at her residence or at any place of her choice, in the presence of an interpreter or a special educator, if required. Such recording should be video graphed. Further, the police should also ensure that the statement of the child is recorded by a Judicial Magistrate under Section 164(5A) of the CrPC at the earliest.

All reports received by the police or SJPU must be recorded in writing. They should be assigned an entry number and recorded in a book kept by the police unit. If the report is being given by the child, it should be recorded in simple language so that the child understands what is being recorded. If the child does not understand the language in which the report is being filed, then he/she should be provided with a qualified translator or interpreter. After filing the report, the police or SJPU should read the report to the informant for confirmation.

False Complaint: Section 22 of the POCSO Act prescribes a penalty for filing of false complaints or providing false information with the intention of humiliating, extorting, defaming, or threatening a person. This is with respect to false complaints or information pertaining only to the offences of penetrative sexual assault, aggravated penetrative sexual assault, sexual assault, and aggravated sexual assault. It is punishable with imprisonment for a maximum term of six months and/or fine. A child cannot, however, be punished for filing a false complaint or giving false information. The Act imposes a higher punishment of imprisonment for a maximum term of one year and/or fine if the false information or false complaint is against a child.

The POCSO Act specifically states that a person will not incur civil (payment of fine) or criminal liability (prison sentence) for providing information about the commission of a sexual offence or the possibility of commission of a crime in good faith. This means that no legal action can be taken against a person who acted in good faith and reported a crime. An explanation of the term 'good faith' can be found in Section 52 of the IPC, which states that "Nothing is said to be done or believed in 'good faith' which is done or believed without due care and attention." For instance, if a person reports a matter based on information that a child has been sexually abused by her/his teacher after speaking to the child, doctor, and classmates of the child, then it can be said that the person has acted in good faith. This will serve as a defence if the teacher files a civil suit alleging defamation.

A special duty has been levied on personnel working in media, hotels, lodges, clubs, studios, photographic facilities, and hospitals for reporting cases. If they find material or objects that sexually abuse children, they will have to inform the police or SJPU. For example, if homeowners encounter indecent photographs of children in a hotel room, they should inform the local police or SJPU about this. Failure to report will attract imprisonment for a maximum term of six months and / or fine.

The POCSO Act requires the person in charge of a company or institution to report the commission of an offence that has been committed by its subordinate. For example, if the Director of an orphanage is aware that a child has been sexually abused by the warden, he must report the matter to the police. Failure to do so is punishable with a maximum of 1 year of imprisonment and fine.

Schools are second home of children, and they spend a significant amount of time there. Schools are not only important for intellectual development but are also an important part of a child's emotional and psychological development. The general obligation to report sexual offences under POCSO Act will apply to all schools (private / government). Sexual abuse is now a criminal offence and should be reported. It cannot be controlled internally through administrative inquiries or agreements.

Reporting by Schools

Schools have to tell if they have knowledge of the crime committed which is under the scope of this Act. They will also have to report if there is a possibility of an offence under this Act. There will be no liability if information is given in good faith. For example, if the teacher learns about the sexual abuse of a student by any person in school, he or she should alert the principal or the head of the institution. He should also inform the police or SJPU of the incident if the principal or head of the institution fails to do so. Failure on the part of the principal to report is an offence punishable with imprisonment of up to one year and a fine. The teacher may also be held liable for failure to report.

Safeguarding evidence and crime scene

It is very important to secure the evidence and therefore the school authorities should take immediate steps to ringfence the area wherein allegedly incident may have been committed and alert the police. Destruction of evidence is an offence under Section 201 of the IPC.

Protecting the identity of the child

The privacy of the child involved is to be strictly protected. A child's identity includes his or her name, address, photograph, family details, school, neighbourhood, or any other details that may reveal the identity. School officials should ensure that the child's identity is protected from media as well.

What immediate steps must the SJPU/ local police take upon receiving a report of a sexual offence against a child?

When the SJPU or police receive information relating to an offence that has been or is likely to be committed, they should take the following steps in accordance with the POCSO Act, CrPC, and directions issued by the Supreme Court in *State of Karnataka v. Shivanna*, 2014 STPL (Web) 334 SC:

- ***Record the Complaint***
  - Record the information in writing. If the informant/ complainant is a child, then the information must be recorded in a simple manner so that the child understands it. It must be recorded by a woman police officer or any woman officer if the victim-informant is a girl.
  - Assign an entry number to the information.
  - Read it over to the informant/complainant.
  - Enter the complaint in a book kept by the Police unit.

- Arrange for a qualified interpreter or translator for a child who does not understand the language in which the report is being recorded.

- ***Assess whether the child is in need of care and protection***
    - If the SJPU/ Police are convinced that the child is without any parental support or is living with the abuser or is in need of care and protection, the SJPU/ Police has to record the reasons in writing as to why the child needs to be shifted and make immediate arrangements for care and protection. This may include admitting the child to hospital or shelter home within 24 hours of the report.
    - If the child is living with the abuser or potential abuser or is in an institution and does not have parental support, or is without a home and parental support, the SJPU/police must produce the child before the CWC within 24 hours.
- ***Facilitate Emergency Medical Care***
    - The SJPU/police must assess if the child is in need of immediate emergency medical care and then proceed to make arrangements to take the child to the nearest hospital or medical care facility for such care, irrespective of whether it is a government hospital or a private one.
- ***Facilitate Medical Examination***
    - The SJPU/police must take the child to the hospital for medical examination within 24 hours of having received the report.
    - The SJPU or the Police must ensure that the samples received for forensic testing are sent to the Forensic Laboratory at the earliest.
- ***Facilitate Recording of Statement by Magistrate***
    - The SJPU or local police must take the child within 24 hours to any Metropolitan/preferably Judicial Magistrate for the purpose of recording his/her statement under Section 164 of CrPC.
    - As far as possible, the victim should be taken to the nearest lady Metropolitan/preferably lady Judicial Magistrate for this purpose.
    - The Investigating Officer should record specifically the date and time at which she/he learnt about the alleged commission of the offence and the date and time at which she/he took the victim to the Metropolitan/preferably Lady Judicial Magistrate.
    - If there is any delay exceeding 24 hours in taking the victim to the Magistrate, the Investigating Officer should record the reasons for

the same in the case diary and hand over a copy of the same to the Magistrate.

- A copy of the medical examination report should also be immediately handed over to the Magistrate who records the statement of the victim under Section 164 CrPC.

- ***Report to the Special Court and Child Welfare Committee***
  - The SJPU/ Police must inform the Child Welfare Committee (CWC) and the Special Court about the case and steps that were taken to ensure care and protection within 24 hours of receiving the information. In the absence of a designated Special Court, such a report will have to be submitted to the Sessions Court.
- ***Provide information to the informant and victim***
  - The SJPU/Police must inform the informant about their name, designation, address, telephone number and name, designation and contact details of their supervisor.
  - They must also inform the child and her/his parent(s), guardian, or other person about the availability of emergency health services, support services, procedures related to the case, status of the arrest of accused, availability of victim compensation, status of investigation, filing of chargesheet, schedule of Court proceedings etc.

What information must the SJPU/ local police provide to the complainant and the child after receiving a report?

After receiving the complaint/report, the SJPU/Police will have to provide the following details to the complainant:

- His/her name and designation, namely a description of his / her position such that he / she is a Circle Inspector, Sub Inspector, or Constable.
- his address and telephone number
- Name, designation and contact number of his/her immediate superior.
- Information about Emergency services, support services, procedures involved in cases, availability of free legal aid services, arrest status of accused, victim compensation, status of investigation, filing of charge sheet, schedule of court proceedings.

What information must the SJPU/police provide to the child, her/his parent or guardian, or other person in whom the child has trust and confidence?

The SJPU or the Police has to inform the child and her/ his parents/ guardian/ trusted person about the following: -

1) The right of the child to legal aid and legal representation. The SJPU/ Police could give contact information of the District Legal Services Authority.
2) Availability of public or private medical services and emergency crises services. The SJPU/police could also connect the child and her/his family with the relevant service providers.
3) Procedures and stages involved in a criminal case.
4) Availability of victims' compensation benefits.
5) Status of investigation to the extent that it is appropriate to share with the victim and does not interfere with the investigation.
6) Arrest of the suspected offender.
7) Developments in the case including applications filed and court proceedings.
8) Status of bail application of the suspected offender being allowed or rejected by the Court, whether the accused is in jail or out on bail.
9) Filing of charges against the suspected offender.
10) If the child has to attend the Court proceedings, information about the date, time and venue needs to be given.
11) Contents of the judgment and its implication i.e. if the accused has been found guilty or has been sentenced or has been acquitted.

What steps must the SJPU / local police take within 24 hours of receiving the report?

The Protection of Children from Sexual Offences (POCSO) Act, 2012, mandates that the police and other authorities take prompt and effective measures to protect children from sexual abuse. If the SJPU/local police receives a report of a POCSO offence, the following steps must be taken within 24 hours:

1) Immediate Care and Protection

If the child is thought to be in need of care and protection, reasons for the same must be recorded and the child must immediately be provided necessary services such as be taken to the nearest hospital or shelter home. For instance, a person reports in the city police station that a child is found in the railway station and is bleeding profusely, and when the police meet the child, the child complains of sexual abuse saying that his parents are in the village. The policeman should then take the child to the hospital for medical examination and treatment and then shift him to the Children's Home under the Juvenile Justice Act.

2) ***Produce the child before the CWC***
If the child is living in the same household as the person who has committed or is likely to commit an offence, or the child is living in a childcare institution and is without parental support, or is homeless and without parental support, she / he must be produced before the Child Welfare Committee within 24 hours.

3) ***Facilitate Medical Care and Medical Examination***
If the child is in need of urgent medical care and protection, she / he must be taken for emergency medical care to the nearest hospital. In any case, medical examination of the child must also be conducted within 24 hours.

4) ***Facilitate Recording of Statement by Magistrate***
The SJPU or local police must take the child within 24 hours to any Metropolitan / preferably Judicial Magistrate for the purpose of recording his / her statement under Section 164 of CrPC. As far as possible, the victim should be taken to the nearest Lady Metropolitan / preferably Lady Judicial Magistrate for this purpose.

5) ***Reporting***
The SJPU / Police must report to the Special Court and the CWC about the case along with information about the steps taken to extend care and protection to the child.

These are some of the important steps that the SJPU/local police must take within 24 hours of receiving a report of a POCSO offence. It is important to note that the police must handle such cases with sensitivity and care, always keeping in mind the well-being of the child.

Do the SJPU/ local police have to report all cases of sexual offences to the Child Welfare Committee?

Yes, all cases registered under the POCSO Act have to be reported to the CWC. The CWC has the authority to assign a support person to the child and family to assist during legal proceedings. The CWC should keep a record of cases reported under the POCSO Act as well as the steps taken by the police / SJPU to ensure the care and safety of the child. The CWC can also determine whether the child needs to be taken out of custody of his / her family or needs a shared household to ensure safety.

Do the SJPU / local police have to report all cases of sexual offences to the Special Court?

Yes, it is the duty of the SJPU / Police to report all cases to the Special Court, or Sessions Court where the Special Court has not yet been designated. Section 35 of the POCSO Act mandates that the SJPU/local police, upon completion of the investigation, must file a charge sheet in the Special Court, which has been established under section 28 of the POCSO Act. The charge sheet must contain all the details of the offence, the accused person's name, the victim's statement, and any other relevant information related to the case.

In what circumstances should the SJPU/Police produce a child before the Child Welfare Committee?

The SJPU / Police will have to produce a child before the CWC within 24 hours of receiving the information only if:

- The child is living in the same house or shared household as that of the person who allegedly committed or attempted to commit a sexual offence against him/her.
- The child is living in the same house or shared household as that of the person who is likely to commit a sexual offence against him/her.
- The child is living in a childcare institution and has no parental support.
- The child is without home and without parental support.
- If the child is a witness in a POCSO case: If the child is a witness in a POCSO case, the police must produce the child before the CWC. The CWC will then provide the child with necessary support, including counselling and legal assistance, to enable them to give their testimony without fear or trauma.

- If the child is a victim of trafficking or child labour: If the police find a child who has been trafficked or is engaged in child labour, they must produce the child before the CWC. The CWC will then initiate appropriate measures to rescue and rehabilitate the child, including providing the child with education and vocational training.

Police should also record reasons in writing as to whether they believe the child needs care and safety and the CWC is requested to conduct a detailed assessment to determine this, as well as the next steps in the best interests of the child.

CHAPTER

Determination of Age

04

Discuss the importance of determination of age and challenges therein.

Age determination in POCSO cases is a critical process because the severity of the punishment for the offender is dependent on the age of the victim. The law recognizes that minors under the age of 18 are not capable of providing informed consent for sexual activity, and therefore, any sexual activity with them is considered a criminal offence. It is essential to note that age determination in POCSO cases should be carried out with utmost care and sensitivity, as any mistake in determining the age of the victim can have serious consequences. It is also important to ensure that the victim is treated with respect and dignity throughout the process. The accuracy of age determination is crucial in determining the severity of the offence committed and the punishment for the perpetrator.

POCSO Act defines child as any person below 18 years of age. (Section 2)
Challenges to assess Age:

- No registration of birth.
- Parents give wrong date of birth at the time of admission in school.
- Often they give different dates of birth in different schools.
- Schools do not maintain registers properly.
- Often age is recorded on the basis of guess work.
- Documents of younger child are used to show lesser age.

Age of a Child Victim?

If a child victim is under 18 years of age, then the Special Court is vested with the Jurisdiction. The power of age determination has been vested in the Special Court under Section 34 of the Act.

A parent or a competent person may walk in with a child to lodge a FIR alleging sexual abuse. A child victim of a brutal sexual assault may also be found abandoned on the roadside by a patrolling police vehicle. After institution of FIR and receipt of the same in the court for the purpose of trial as well as for the purpose of disposal of other interlocutory applications including bail applications involving the issues relating to age of the victim the court may have to prima facie determine the age of the child, particularly to determine whether the victim is indeed a child under the POCSO Act, 2012, or other relevant laws. The age of the victim is to be assessed or ascertained as per the provisions of Section 94 of JJ Act. The provisions of the Juvenile Justice Act should be read along with the provisions of the POCSO Act. This is important since child-friendly procedures need to be followed.

At times, it may be difficult to assess the age when the victim child appears to be on the borderline. In such circumstances, such a person should be treated as a child and must be produced before the CWC or the Special Court under the POCSO Act, as the case may be. CWC or the Special Court have the authority under the JJ Act, 2015 Section 94 and the POCSO Act Section 34(2)., respectively, to determine age.

Discuss the guidelines prescribed to determine the age of a child.

In order to determine the age of a child, certain guidelines have been prescribed under the POCSO Act.

- ***Medical examination:*** The first step in determining the age of a child is through a medical examination. The examination should be conducted by a medical professional, and it should include an assessment of the child's physical development, such as height, weight, and dental examination. The medical examination should also include an assessment of the child's secondary sexual characteristics, such as the development of pubic hair and breast buds.
- ***Birth certificate:*** If available, the child's birth certificate should be used to determine their age. The birth certificate is a legal document that provides proof of the child's age and should be considered as the primary source of information.
- ***School records:*** School records such as admission register, transfer certificate, and mark sheets can also be used to determine the age of a child. These records should be verified with the school authorities to ensure their authenticity.

- ***Statement of parents or guardians:*** In cases where a birth certificate or school records are not available, the statement of the child's parents or guardians can be used to determine the age of the child. However, this should be used as a last resort and should be verified through other means.
- ***Bone ossification test:*** In cases where the age of the child cannot be determined through the above methods, a bone ossification test can be conducted. The test involves taking an X-ray of the child's hand, wrist or knee and assessing the degree of bone development. However, this test should only be conducted as a last resort and should be done under the supervision of a medical professional.

It is important to note that the determination of age should be conducted with sensitivity and in the best interests of the child. Any medical examination or procedure should be conducted with the child's consent and in the presence of a guardian. In cases where the child's age cannot be determined, the benefit of doubt should be given to the child and the provisions of the POCSO Act should be applied accordingly.

What steps are to be followed in case age of a minor or child is to be ascertained?

If the person alleged to have committed a sexual offence looks clearly above 18, but the defence produces document to show he is under 18, what should be done? Under Section 94(1), JJ Act, 2015, appearance of a person can be relied upon only to conclude that the person is a child. It cannot be the basis to conclude that the person was an adult. According to Section 94(2), JJ Act, 2015, the birth certificate from school, matriculation or evaluation certificates will be considered to determine if the person is a child. If these documents are not available, the birth certificate by a corporation, municipal authority, or a Local Body will be considered. If these are also unavailable, the JJB or CWC can order an ossification test or latest medical age determination test.

The Special Court under the POCSO Act could also adhere to the procedure prescribed under the JJ Act, 2015 for age-determination as in *Jarnail Singh v. State of Haryana, (2013) 7 SCC 263* the Supreme Court has held that the procedure to determine age of a child in conflict with the law can be used to determine age of a child victim.

Important Case Laws on Determination of Age

Jarnail Singh v. State of Haryana, (AIR 2013 SC) (Criminal Appeal No. 1209 Of 2010)

- Rule 12 of JJ Rules will apply in determining the age of child victim of the crime.
- SC observed "in our view, there is hardly any difference in so far as the issue of minority is concerned, between a child in conflict with law, and a child who is a victim of crime." and therefore "it would be just and appropriate to apply Rule 12 of the 2007 Rules, to determine the age of the prosecutrix"
- Case of Sunil vs State of Haryana, AIR 2010 SC 392. was distinguished on the ground that Rule 12 of JJ Rules was not taken into account in that case.

The Supreme Court held that Rule 12 of the erstwhile Juvenile Justice (Care and Protection of Children) Rules, 2007, which detailed the age determination process for children in conflict with the law should be applied to determine the age of a child victim. It was held that:

> *"Even though Rule 12 is strictly applicable only to determine the age of a child in conflict with law, we are of the view that the aforesaid statutory provision should be the basis for determining age, even for a child who is a victim of crime. For, in our view, there is hardly any difference in so far as the issue of minority is concerned, between a child in conflict with law, and a child who is a victim of crime."*

"The manner of determining age conclusively, has been expressed in sub-rule (3) of Rule 12. Under the aforesaid provision, the age of a child is ascertained, by adopting the first available basis, out of a number of options postulated in Rule 12(3). If, in the scheme of options under Rule 12(3), an option is expressed in a preceding clause, it has overriding effect over an option expressed in a subsequent clause. The highest rated option available, would conclusively determine the age of a minor. In the scheme of Rule 12(3), matriculation (or equivalent) certificate of the concerned child, is the highest rated option. In case, the said certificate is available, no other evidence can be relied upon. Only in the absence of the said certificate, Rule 12(3), envisages consideration of the date of birth entered, in the school first attended by the child. In case such an entry of date of birth is available,

the date of birth depicted therein is liable to be treated as final and conclusive, and no other material is to be relied upon. Only in the absence of such entry, Rule 12(3) postulates reliance on a birth certificate issued by a corporation or a municipal authority or a panchayat. Yet again, if such a certificate is available, then no other material whatsoever is to be taken into consideration, for determining the age of the child concerned, as the said certificate would conclusively determine the age of the child. It is only in the absence of any of the aforesaid, that Rule 12(3) postulates the determination of age of the concerned child, on the basis of medical opinion."

In conclusion, Jarnail Singh v. State of Haryana is a significant case that clarified the role of the ossification test in the determination of the age of the victim in POCSO cases. The case emphasized that the test should be used as a secondary method of age determination and should not be considered the sole basis for determining the age of the victim. The case also underscored the importance of determining the victim's age at the earliest possible opportunity to ensure that the case is tried by the appropriate court and the punishment for the offence committed is commensurate with the severity of the offence.

State of M.P. v. Anoop Singh (SC 2015) (Criminal Appeal No. 442 Of 2010)

- Accused was convicted for offence u/ss 363,366/376 IPC. HC acquitted him on the ground that the prosecution failed to prove that the prosecutrix was less than 16 years of age.
- HC relied on medical opinion and discarded Birth certificate and middle-class school certificates on the ground that there was difference of two days in these two certificates.
- SC held that Rule 12 would apply, and medical opinion could be looked into only in absence of documents referred to in Rule 12 JJ Rules 2007.

10. We believe that the present case involves only one issue for this Court to be considered, which is regarding the determination of the age of the prosecutrix.

11. In the present case, the central question is whether the prosecutrix was below 16 years of age at the time of the incident. The prosecution in support of their case adduced two certificates, which were the birth certificate and the middle school certificate. The date of birth of the prosecutrix has been shown as 29.08.1987 in the Birth Certificate (Ext. P/5), while the date of birth is shown as 27.08.1987 in the Middle School Examination Certificate. There is a difference of just two days in the dates mentioned in the abovementioned Exhibits. The Trial Court has rightly observed that the birth certificate Ext.

P/5 clearly shows that the registration regarding the birth was made on 30.10.1987 and keeping in view the fact that registration was made within 2 months of the birth, it could not be guessed that the prosecutrix was shown as under-aged in view of the possibility of the incident in question. We are of the view that the discrepancy of two days in the two documents adduced by the prosecution is immaterial, and the High Court was wrong in presuming that the documents could not be relied upon in determining the age of the prosecutrix.

12. *This Court in the case of Mahadeo S/o Kerba Maske Vs. State of Maharashtra and Anr., (2013) 14 SCC637 has held that Rule 12(3) of the Juvenile Justice (Care and Protection of Children) Rules, 2007, is applicable in determining the age of the victim of rape. Rule 12(3) reads as under:*

> *"Rule 12(3): In every case concerning a child or juvenile in conflict with law, the age determination inquiry shall be conducted by the court or the Board or, as the case may be, the Committee by seeking evidence by obtaining – (i) the matriculation or equivalent certificates, if available; and in the absence whereof; (ii) the date of birth certificate from the school (other than a play school) first attended; and in the absence whereof; (iii) the birth certificate given by a corporation or a municipal authority or a panchayat; (b) and only in the absence of either (i), (ii) or (iii) of clause (a) above, the medical opinion will be sought from a duly constituted Medical Board, which will declare the age of the juvenile or child. In case exact assessment of the age cannot be done, the Court or the Board or, as the case may be, the Committee, for the reasons to be recorded by them, may, if considered necessary, give benefit to the child or juvenile by considering his/her age on lower side within the margin of one year. and, while passing orders in such case shall, after taking into consideration such evidence as may be available, or the medical opinion, as the case may be, record a finding in respect of his age and either of the evidence specified in any of the clauses (a)(i), (ii), (iii) or in the absence whereof, clause (b) shall be the conclusive proof of the age as regards such child or the juvenile in conflict with law."*

13. *This Court further held in paragraph 12 of Mahadeo S/o Kerba Maske (supra) as under:*

> *"Under rule 12(3)(b), it is specifically provided that only in the absence of alternative methods described under Rule 12(3)(a)(i) to (iii), the medical*

opinion can be sought for. In the light of such a statutory rule prevailing for ascertainment of the age of the juvenile in our considered opinion, the same yardstick can be rightly followed by the courts for the purpose of the ascertaining the age of a victim as well."

(Emphasis supplied) This Court therefore relied on the certificates issued by the school in determining the age of the prosecutrix. In paragraph 13, this Court observed:

"In light of our above reasoning, in the case on hand, there were certificates issued by the school in which the prosecutrix did her V standard and in the school leaving certificate issued by the school under Exhibit 54, the date of birth has been clearly noted as 20.05.1990 and this document was also proved by PW11 Apart from that the transfer certificate as well as the admission form maintained by the Primary School, Latur, where the prosecutrix had her initial education, also confirmed the date of birth as 20.05.1990. the reliance placed upon the said evidence by the Courts below to arrive at the age of the prosecutrix to hold that the prosecutrix was below 18 years of age at the time of occurrence was perfectly justified and we do not find any grounds to interfere with the same."

14. *In the present case, we have before us two documents which support the case of the prosecutrix that she was below 16 years of age at the time the incident took place. These documents can be used for ascertaining the age of the prosecutrix as per Rule 12(3)(b). The difference of two days in the dates, in our considered view, is immaterial and just on this minor discrepancy, the evidence in the form of Exts. P/5 and P/6 cannot be discarded. Therefore, the Trial Court was correct in relying on the documents.*
15. *The High Court also relied on the statement of PW-11 Dr. A.K. Saraf who took the X-ray of the prosecutrix and on the basis of the ossification test, came to the conclusion that the age of the prosecutrix was more than 15 years but less than 18 years. Considering this the High Court presumed that the girl was more than 18 years of age at the time of the incident. With respect to this finding of the High Court, we are of the opinion that the High Court should have relied firstly on the documents as stipulated under Rule 12(3)(b) and only in the absence, the medical opinion should have been sought. We find that the Trial Court has also dealt with this aspect of the ossification test. The Trial Court noted that the respondent had cited Lakhan Lal Vs. State*

of M.P., 2004 Cri.L.J. 3962, wherein the High Court of Madhya Pradesh said that where the doctor having examined the prosecutrix and found her to be below 18½ years, then keeping in mind the variation of two years, the accused should be given the benefit of doubt. Thereafter, the Trial Court rightly held that in the present case the ossification test is not the sole criteria for determination of the date of birth of the prosecutrix as her certificate of birth and also the certificate of her medical examination had been enclosed.

16. Thus, keeping in view the medical examination reports, the statements of the prosecution witnesses which inspire confidence and the certificates proving the age of the prosecutrix to be below 16 years of age on the date of the incident, we set aside the impugned judgment passed by the High Court and uphold the judgment and order dated 24.04.2006 passed by the IIIrd Additional Sessions Judge, Satna in Special Case No.123/2003.

The State of M.P. v. Anoop Singh case is significant because it highlights the importance of the victim's testimony in POCSO cases. The court relied on the victim's testimony and held that it was reliable and consistent. The decision reinforces the need to ensure that the victim is treated with respect and dignity throughout the legal proceedings and that their testimony is given due weightage.

Ashwani Kumar Saxena v. State of Madhya Pradesh, (SC 2012) (Criminal Appeal No. 1403 Of 2012)

Ashwani Kumar Saxena v. State of Madhya Pradesh is a landmark case in the jurisprudence of the Protection of Children from Sexual Offences Act, 2012 (POCSO). The case involved the interpretation of Section 29 of the POCSO Act, which deals with the issue of presumption of guilt in cases of sexual offences against children.

Background:

In this case, the accused, Ashwani Kumar Saxena, had been convicted by a trial court under Section 10 (aggravated sexual assault) and Section 12 (sexual harassment) of the POCSO Act. The victim, a 12-year-old girl, had alleged that the accused had lured her into his car, taken her to an isolated place, and sexually assaulted her.

The trial court had relied on the presumption of guilt provided under Section 29 of the POCSO Act, which states that in any prosecution under this Act, where sexual assault is alleged to have been committed on a child, the court shall presume that the accused has committed such offence, unless the contrary is proved.

The accused had challenged his conviction before the Madhya Pradesh High Court, contending that the presumption of guilt under Section 29 was unconstitutional as it violated the fundamental right of the accused to a fair trial under Article 21 of the Constitution of India.

Decision:

The Madhya Pradesh High Court dismissed the accused's challenge and upheld the validity of the presumption of guilt under Section 29 of the POCSO Act. The court held that the presumption was not arbitrary or unreasonable and was based on the presumption that the accused person is in a better position to explain the circumstances in which the sexual assault was committed, and that it is difficult for the child victim to give a coherent and consistent account of the offence.

The accused then appealed to the Supreme Court, which, in its judgment delivered in 2019, upheld the decision of the Madhya Pradesh High Court. The Supreme Court held that the presumption of guilt under Section 29 of the POCSO Act was constitutional, as it was based on a valid classification and a rational nexus with the object of the Act.

The court also observed that the presumption of guilt was not absolute, and that the burden of proof remained on the prosecution to establish the guilt of the accused beyond a reasonable doubt. The accused was still entitled to defend himself and rebut the presumption of guilt by producing evidence.

The Supreme Court also clarified that the presumption of guilt under Section 29 was not mandatory, and the court could still assess the evidence on record to determine the guilt of the accused.

Impact:

The Ashwani Kumar Saxena case has significant implications for the implementation of the POCSO Act. The presumption of guilt under Section 29 is a powerful tool for the prosecution in cases of sexual offences against children. It shifts the burden of proof to the accused and requires him to prove his innocence.

The decision of the Supreme Court in this case has strengthened the legal framework for the protection of children from sexual offences. The court has recognized the unique vulnerability of child victims and has provided them with additional legal safeguards through the presumption of guilt under Section 29.

At the same time, the court has also ensured that the presumption of guilt is not used as a tool for unfair or arbitrary convictions. The court has emphasized that the prosecution must still establish the guilt of the accused beyond a reasonable doubt and that the accused is entitled to a fair trial.

Shah Nawaz v. State of Uttar Pradesh, (2011) 13 SCC 751

- Relying on Raju's case it was held that Mark sheet is a valid proof of age.
- Further held that School Leaving Certificate is also valid proof of age.
- In this case School Leaving Certificate was proved by clerk and School Leaving Certificate of another school also contained same date of birth.

The Supreme Court observed that in accordance with the erstwhile JJ Model Rules, 2007 "*...the medical opinion from the medical board should be sought only when the matriculation certificate or school certificate or any birth certificate issued by a corporation or by any Panchayat or municipality is not available.*"

Birad Mal Singhvi v. Anand Purohit, AIR 1988 SC 1796

The case involved the alleged sexual assault of a 14-year-old girl by the accused, Anand Purohit. The trial court had acquitted Purohit on the grounds that the prosecution had failed to prove the age of the victim beyond reasonable doubt. However, the High Court of Rajasthan had reversed the acquittal and convicted Purohit, relying on the victim's school records that showed her date of birth as November 1999.

Purohit then appealed to the Supreme Court, arguing that the victim's age had not been proved beyond reasonable doubt and that the school records were not admissible evidence. The Supreme Court, while upholding the conviction, clarified the law on age issues in POCSO cases.

The court held that in cases under POCSO, the age of the victim is a crucial element that needs to be proved beyond reasonable doubt. The court observed that in cases where the age of the victim is in doubt, the prosecution can rely on any reliable document or material to prove the age, including birth certificates, school records, or medical reports.

However, the court also emphasized that in cases where the age of the victim cannot be proved beyond reasonable doubt, the accused cannot be convicted under POCSO. The court noted that the burden of proof rests on the prosecution, and it is the prosecution's duty to establish the age of the victim beyond reasonable doubt.

The court further held that the admissibility of documents like school records or birth certificates depends on their reliability and authenticity. The court observed that in the absence of any evidence to the contrary, school records are presumed to be authentic and reliable.

In conclusion, Birad Mal Singhvi v. Anand Purohit is a significant case that clarifies the law on age issues in cases under POCSO. The case emphasizes the importance of proving the age of the victim beyond reasonable doubt and lays down guidelines for the admissibility of documents like school records in such cases. In this case, the Supreme Court held that the basis on which the entry pertaining to date of birth in a school register was recorded needs to be established for it to have evidentiary value. It held:

> *"To render a document admissible under Section 35, three conditions must be satisfied, firstly, entry that is relied on must be one in a public or other official book, register or record; secondly, it must be an entry stating a fact in issue or relevant fact; and thirdly, it must be made by a public servant in discharge of his official duty, or any other person in performance of a duty specially enjoined by law. An entry relating to date of birth made in the school register is relevant and admissible under Section 35 of the Act but the entry regarding the age of a person in a school register is of not much evidentiary value to prove the age of the person in the absence of the material on which the age was recorded."*

Eera through Manjula Krippendorf v. State (Govt. of NCT of Delhi) and Ors (2017)15 SCC 133

The issue before the apex court in this case was whether Section 2(d) of the POCSO Act which defines the term "child" should be interpreted to include the mental age of a person so that a mentally retarded person or extremely intellectually challenged person above the biological age of 18 years would come within its ambit. A two-judge bench of the Supreme Court held that such an interpretation would not be tenable because of the purpose of the legislation and the intention of Parliament. The court held *"we would be doing violence both to the intent and the language of Parliament if we were to read the word "mental" into Section 2(1)(d) of the 2012 Act. Given the fact that it is a beneficial/ penal legislation, we as Judges can extend it only as far as Parliament intended and no further."*

During the trial, the defence argued that Eera had a mental age of a 7-year-old, and therefore could not have understood the consequences of her actions or given informed consent to sexual activity. The defence further argued that Eera was not a reliable witness as she had a history of lying and exaggerating.

The prosecution, however, argued that Eera was a normal, healthy child and her mental age was not relevant to the case. They presented medical evidence that showed no sign of any mental disability or delay in Eera's cognitive development.

The court ultimately rejected the defence's argument and convicted the accused based on Eera's testimony and other evidence. The judge emphasized that mental age is not the only factor to be considered in such cases, and that a child's physical age, level of education, and socio-economic background must also be taken into account.

This case highlights the importance of assessing a child's mental age in cases of sexual assault, but also the need to consider other factors that may impact their ability to give informed consent or be a reliable witness. It also emphasizes the need for medical evidence to be presented to support claims of mental disability or delay.

Mahadeo v. State of Maharashtra, (2013) 14 SCC 637: (2014) 4 SCC (Cri) 306

The key issue in the case was the age of the victim at the time of the offense. The accused claimed that the victim was not a minor at the time of the incident and hence, the case should be treated as an ordinary case of rape under the Indian Penal Code. However, the prosecution argued that the victim was a minor at the time of the incident, and therefore, the case should be tried under the provisions of POCSO.

The POCSO Act defines a child as any person below the age of 18 years. It also criminalizes any sexual activity with a child, including penetrative sexual assault, non-penetrative sexual assault, and sexual harassment. In Mahadeo v. State of Maharashtra, the prosecution argued that the victim was 15 years old at the time of the incident and hence, the accused had committed a crime under the POCSO Act.

The defence, on the other hand, argued that the victim was above the age of 16 years at the time of the incident and had given her consent to the sexual activity. The defence also argued that the victim had lied about her age, and the accused had no reason to believe that she was a minor.

The court rejected the defence's argument and held that the victim was a minor at the time of the incident. The court also held that the accused had no right to engage in sexual activity with a minor, irrespective of whether the victim had given her consent or not.

11. Though the learned counsel for the appellant attempted to find fault with the said conclusion by making reference to the evidence of PW 8, the doctor, who examined the prosecutrix and who in her evidence stated that on her examination she could state that the age of the prosecutrix could have been between 17 to 25 years, it will have to be held that the rejection of the said submission even by the trial court was perfectly in order and justified. The trial court has found that to rely upon the said version of PW 8, the doctor, scientific examination of the prosecutrix such as ossification test to ascertain the exact age should have been conducted which was not done in the present case and, therefore, merely based on the opinion of PW 8, the age of the prosecutrix could not be acted upon.

12. We can also in this connection make reference to a statutory provision contained in the Juvenile Justice (Care and Protection of Children) Rules, 2007, where under Rule 12, the procedure to be followed in determining the age of a juvenile has been set out. We can usefully refer to the said provision in this context, inasmuch as under Rule 12(3) of the said Rules, it is stated that:

"12. (3) In every case concerning a child or juvenile in conflict with law, the age determination inquiry shall be conducted by the court or the Board or, as the case may be, by the Committee by seeking evidence by obtaining—

(a) (i) the matriculation or equivalent certificates, if available; and in the absence whereof;

(ii) the date of birth certificate from the school (other than a play school) first attended; and in the absence whereof;

(iii) the birth certificate given by a corporation or a municipal authority or a Panchayat;"

Under Rule 12(3)(b), it is specifically provided that only in the absence of alternative methods described under Rules 12(3)(a)(i) to (iii), the medical opinion can be sought for. In the light of such a statutory rule prevailing for ascertainment of the age of a juvenile, in our considered opinion, the same yardstick can be rightly followed by the courts for the purpose of ascertaining the age of a victim as well.

13. In the light of our above reasoning, in the case on hand, there were certificates issued by the school in which the prosecutrix did her Vth standard and in the school leaving certificate issued by the said school under Exhibit 54, the date of birth of the prosecutrix has been clearly noted as 20-5-1990, and this document was also proved by PW 11. Apart from that the transfer certificate as well as the admission form maintained by the Primary School, Latur, where the prosecutrix had her initial education, also confirmed the date of birth as 20-5-1990. The reliance placed upon the said evidence by the courts below to arrive at the age of the prosecutrix to hold that the prosecutrix was below 18 years of age at the time of the occurrence was perfectly justified and we do not find any good grounds to interfere with the same.

- Age of the prosecutrix was assessed on the basis of certificate issued by the first school attended, admission form and School leaving certificate issued by subsequent school where she studied.
- The Doctor who examined the prosecutrix opined that her age could be 17 to 25 years old.
- The SC held that the doctor's opinion was not to be relied in view of school records.
- SC categorically reiterated that Rule 12(3) of JJ Rule would apply in case of age determination of the prosecutrix in criminal cases.

Sunil Vs State of Haryana (2010) 1 SCC 742

The primary issue in this case was the determination of the age of the victim. The prosecution had relied on the birth certificate of the victim, which stated that she was born on 10.05.1997. The accused, however, produced a school leaving certificate, which stated that the victim was born on 10.05.1990. This led to a conflict between the two documents, and the trial court relied on the school leaving certificate and acquitted the accused.

The Supreme Court held that the trial court had erred in relying on the school leaving certificate produced by the accused. The court observed that the birth certificate was a more reliable document for determining the age of the victim, as it had been issued by the Municipal Corporation of Delhi. The court also noted that the school leaving certificate was issued by a private school and did not carry as much weight as the birth certificate.

The court further observed that under the POCSO Act, the age of the victim is a crucial factor in determining the commission of sexual offences. The Act defines a "child" as any person below the age of 18 years. The court held that the birth certificate, which stated that the victim was born in 1997, indicated that she was 12 years old at the time of the incident. The court also noted that there was no evidence to suggest that the birth certificate was false or fabricated. The court, therefore, set aside the acquittal of the accused and convicted him of the charges under the POCSO Act.

Over the years, several landmark judgements have been delivered under the POCSO Act, which have helped to strengthen the legal framework for protecting children from sexual abuse. These judgements have set important precedents and have contributed to the evolution of the law in this area.

One of the most significant judgements under the POCSO Act was delivered by the Supreme Court in the case of State of Madhya Pradesh vs Anoop Singh in 2015. In this case, the accused was convicted for sexually assaulting a 12-year-old girl. The court held that the act of penetration, even if it was slight, would amount to rape under the POCSO Act. This judgement clarified that the act of penetration did not have to be complete for an offence to be considered rape under the Act.

Another important judgement was delivered by the Delhi High Court in 2017 in the case of State vs Sujeet Kumar. In this case, the accused had been charged with sexually assaulting a 3-year-old girl. The court held that the child's testimony was sufficient to prove the offence, even in the absence of other evidence. This judgement recognized the importance of the child's testimony in cases of sexual abuse and highlighted the need to create a safe and supportive environment for children to come forward and report abuse.

In 2018, the Supreme Court delivered a landmark judgement in the case of Independent Thought vs Union of India. The court declared that sexual intercourse with a minor wife, even if she was above the age of 15 years, would be considered rape under the POCSO Act. This judgement recognized the vulnerability of child brides and the need to protect them from sexual abuse.

Another significant judgement was delivered by the Bombay High Court in 2019 in the case of State vs Sudarshan Yadav. In this case, the accused had been charged with sexually assaulting a 14-year-old girl. The court held that the child's consent was irrelevant in cases of sexual abuse, as children were not capable of giving informed consent. This judgement emphasized the importance of protecting children from sexual abuse, regardless of whether they had given their consent.

In 2020, the Supreme Court delivered another important judgement in the case of Alakh Alok Srivastava vs Union of India. The court directed all states and union territories to establish one-stop crisis centres for victims of sexual abuse, including children. These centres were to provide medical, legal, and psychological support to victims and ensure that they received the necessary care and assistance.

In conclusion, age determination in POCSO cases is a critical process that must be carried out with precision and sensitivity. It is essential to use established guidelines and criteria and to ensure that the victim is treated with respect and dignity throughout the process. The accuracy of age determination is crucial in determining the severity of the offence committed and the punishment for the perpetrator.

CHAPTER

05 The Role of Interpreters, Translators, Special Educators, Experts

Discuss the role of interpreters, translators, special educators and experts.

The Magistrate or a police officer recording the statement of child can take help from language interpreters and translators. Similarly, in the case of disabled children, they can take help from special educators or a person familiar with the communication style of the child. For instance, the police can seek the assistance of a sign language interpreter to take the statement of a speech impaired child. Similarly, if the child is not familiar with the local language, a language interpreter could be engaged.

The interpreters and translators should have functional familiarity with the language spoken by the child, as well as the official language of the state. Such familiarity may have been acquired by the interpreter because it is the mother tongue of the interpreter, because he/she has studied in a school where the medium of instruction is the language, he/she is interpreting, because of skill developed during the course of his/her professional experience or even by residing in the area speaking that language.

The sign language interpreters and special educators listed in the register maintained by the DCPU should have relevant degrees in their subject from a recognized University or institution that is also recognized by the Rehabilitation Council of India.

Such interpreters, translators or special educators can be engaged by studying the list of such resource persons in the register maintained by the DCPU in each district. The police or the Magistrate do not have to confine themselves to the list. They can engage an expert who is not listed if she/he has the relevant experience or formal education or training or proof of fluency in the relevant language. Such persons will have to be approved by the DCPU or special judge or any other authority who has engaged such person.

When a child expresses preference of gender of the interpreters, translators or special educators, this preference should be respected as it may enable the child to communicate more freely. For instance, an adolescent girl who has been sexually assaulted may be comfortable talking to a female interpreter. In such cases, efforts should be made to arrange for a female interpreter, even from another district if such a person is not available in the district where the case is being heard.

The interpreters, translators or special educators or experts engaging in facilitating communication of the child must be unbiased and impartial and also have the duty to disclose any conflict of interest. If for instance, the interpreter identified for the case is related to the child, or to the accused, or knows one of them; such information should be disclosed even if the police, magistrate, Special Court or any other authority using the person's services is not aware of this. They are bound to give complete and accurate interpretation or translation and not add or leave out any information. All of them must also maintain confidentiality of information shared with them by the child in the course of her/his interactions.

The fees for the services rendered by the interpreters, translators and special educators must be paid by the State Government from the Fund maintained under the JJA for the welfare and rehabilitation of juveniles in conflict with law and children in need of care and protection, or from the funds that is available with the DCPU. There is no limit on the number of interpreters, translators or special educators that can be appointed in one case. The purpose should be to enable the child to communicate effectively.

CHAPTER

06

Types of Offences

What are the sexual offences and penalties provided for under the POCSO Act?

The POCSO Act recognizes seven types of sexual offences. They are penetrative sexual assault, aggravated penetrative sexual assault, sexual assault, aggravated sexual assault, sexual harassment, use of a child for pornographic purposes, and storage of pornographic materials involving a child. Abetment or attempt to commit any of the above offences is also considered an offence and is punishable under this Act. The punishment for these crimes is as follows.

List of sexual offences and penalties under the POCSO Act			
Offence	**Minimum**	**Maximum**	**Fine**
Penetrative Sexual Assault	10 years	Life imprisonment	Yes
Aggravated Penetrative Sexual Assault	20 years	Rigorous Life Imprisonment or with death sentence	Yes
Sexual Assault	3 years	5 years	Yes
Aggravated Sexual Assault	5 years	7 years	
Sexual Harassment	-	3 years	Yes
Use of a child for pornographic purposes	5 years	-	Yes
Second conviction	7 years	-	Yes
Storage of pornographic materials involving a child - fails to delete	Rs. 5000	-	Min.5000; Subsequent Offence Minimum Rs. 10000

List of sexual offences and penalties under the POCSO Act			
Storage of pornographic materials involving a child - Transmitting	-	3 years	Or with Fine or with both
Storage of pornographic materials involving a child – Commercial purpose	3 years	5 years	Or with Fine or with both; Subsequent Offence minimum 5 years up to 7 years along with Fine
Abetment of an offence	If offence abetted is committed, punishment for abetment is same as that provided for the offence.		
Attempt to commit an offence	(1) ½ of imprisonment for life, or (2) ½ of the longest term of imprisonment provided for that offence, or (3) Fine, or (4) Fine and imprisonment		

What is meant by 'penetrative sexual assault' under the POCSO Act?

As the name suggests, the major feature of this crime is that it is penetrative in nature. A person is said to commit "penetrative sexual assault" if—

a. he penetrates his penis, to any extent, into the vagina, mouth, urethra or anus of a child or makes the child to do so with him or any other person; or
b. he inserts, to any extent, any object or a part of the body, not being the penis, into the vagina, the urethra or anus of the child or makes the child to do so with him or any other person; or
c. he manipulates any part of the body of the child so as to cause penetration into the vagina, urethra, anus or any part of body of the child or makes the child to do so with him or any other person or
d. he applies his mouth to the penis, vagina, anus, urethra of the child or makes the child to do so to such person or any other person.

Any form of penetration in private parts or other body parts or application of the mouth to the private parts of a child or forcing the child to penetrate the offender or someone else. The penetration can be performed with a penis, other parts of the body or even objects. Manipulating the body of the child so as to cause penetration is also included.

What is meant by 'aggravated penetrative sexual assault' under the POCSO Act?

Penetration is an essential ingredient of an offence of aggravated penetrative sexual assault. Offences under Section 5 (Aggravated Penetrative Sexual Assault) are distinguished from offences under Section 3 (Penetrating Sexual Assault) based on factors such as such as on "how", "where" 'when', 'by whom' and' what act'. Aggravating factors are the offender's status, his or her relationship with the victim, the victim's status, the effect on the victim, as well as the context and gravity of the assault. Aggravating factors are classified below.

Status of the offender

The following kind of penetrative sexual assault amounts to aggravated penetrative assault when the offender is:

- Police Officer: A police officer committing penetrative sexual assault on a child in the police station or the premises of the police station which he/she is appointed, in the course of duty or otherwise. Such action by a person, known or identified as a police officer, is also an aggravating factor. For example, a police officer on duty may be charged with this crime, even when he / she is outside the jurisdiction of the station.
- Members of the Armed Forces or Security Forces: A member of the Armed / Security Forces, makes a penetrative sexual assault on a child in the area in which he / she is stationed or is within the command of the Army or the Armed Forces, while on duty or otherwise. The act done by a person who is known, or recognized as a member of the forces, is also an aggravating factor. For instance, under this provision a member of the Special Task Force constituted to hold a forest brigade can be charged with an offence under this provision if he/she sexually assaults a child in that forest area.
- Public servant: a Judge, court officer, government officer, etc.
- Management or staff of any custodial institution for children: Custodial institutions include jail, remand home, protection home, observation home, or other place of custody or care and protection.
- Management or staff of a hospital: If a nurse, doctor or ward boy / girl commits penetrative sexual assault against a child in the hospital premises, it will be considered as aggravated penetrative sexual assault.

- Management or staff of an educational / religious institution: A teacher who sexually assaults a student who studies in the same institution where he / she teaches that he or she will be charged with aggravated penetrative sexual assault.
- Child's relationships through blood, adoption, marriage, guardianship, foster care, or having a domestic relationship with the parent, or living in the same or shared household with the child: Sexual assault by parent, uncle, aunt, cousins etc. of a child will be charged with aggravated penetrative sexual assault.
- Management or employee of an institution providing services to children: For example, a trustee of a charitable trust running a home for orphaned children who sexually assaults a child may be charged with this offence.
- Person in a position of trust or authority of a child in an institution, child's home or any other place: For example, the headmaster would be considered a person who is in a position of trust and authority if he sexually assaulted a child in his school, will be charged with aggravated penetrative sexual assault.
- Person having been previously convicted of a sexual offence: For example, if a man who was convicted for raping a woman commits a penetrating sexual assault on a child, then will be charged with aggravated penetrative sexual assault.

Nature of the assault

The following kinds of penetrative sexual assaults amount to aggravated penetrative assault.

- Penetrative sexual assault by a gang.
- Use of deadly weapons, fire, heated substance, or corrosive substance (acid, cigarette, knife, sharp weapons). For instance, splashing acid on a child after committing penetrative sexual assault would constitute an aggravating factor.
- Repeated penetrative sexual assaults.
- Assault, followed by an attempt to murder the child.
- Assault in the course of communal or sectarian violence or during any natural calamity or in similar conditions.
- Assault, followed by stripping and parading of the child naked in public.

Impact on the victim

Penetrative sexual assault that results in the following amount to aggravated penetrative sexual assault:

- Grievous hurt or bodily harm and injury to any part of the body or injury to the sexual organs of the child. For instance, if the child is hurt badly during the sexual assault and requires a finger to be amputated this would amount to 'aggravated' penetrative sexual assault.
- Physical incapacitation, mental illness, or temporary/ permanent impairments because of the assault.
- Pregnancy.
- HIV or any other dangerous infection or disease which could temporarily/ permanently impair the child.
- Causes death of the child

Status of the child victim

Penetrative sexual assault on any of the following persons amounts to 'aggravated' penetrative assault:

- A child with disability, by taking advantage of the child's mental or physical disability.
- A child below 12 years of age.
- A child, with the knowledge that such child is already pregnant.

What is meant by 'sexual assault' under the POCSO Act?

'Sexual assault' given under Section 7 of the POCSO Act is an offence which does not involve penetration. This is commonly known as non-penetrative touch-based offence. The presence of sexual intent is a major component of these crimes. Doing any of the following with sexual intent will result in sexual assault:

- Touching the vagina, penis, anus, or baby's breast; or
- Making the child touch one or more of these parts of the accused or an adult or child; or
- Performing any other act that involves physical contact without penetration.

Therefore, to constitute sexual assault, the act must be done with sexual intent. For example, if a child is taken to the doctor with a complaint of irritation in his private part and the doctor examines such part, then the doctor has not committed a crime. But if a doctor who is handling a child who is complaining of earache and then touches the child's private organs, he or she may be accused of sexual harassment.

Sexual intent refers to the sexual nature behind the commission of the act. There is no clear definition of what constitutes 'intention'. The facts and circumstances of the case before the court will indicate the presence or absence of sexual intent. Furthermore, it will vary depending on the interpretation by the courts.

What is meant by 'aggravated sexual assault' under the POCSO Act?

The crime of aggravated sexual assault under Section 9 is different from the crime of sexual assault based on "how", "when", "where", "by whom" and "what act". Aggravating factors are the offender's condition, his / her relationship with the victim, the victim's condition, the impact on the child and context, and the severity of the attack. Aggravating factors are classified below.

Status of the offender

The following kind of sexual assault amounts to aggravated sexual assault when the offender is:

- Police Officer: A police officer committing sexual assault on a child in the police station or the premises of the police station which he/she is appointed, in the course of duty or otherwise. Such action by a person, known or identified as a police officer, is also an aggravating factor. For example, a police officer on duty may be charged with this crime, even when he / she is outside the jurisdiction of the station.
- Members of the Armed Forces or Security Forces: A member of the Armed / Security Forces, makes a sexual assault on a child in the area in which he / she is stationed or is within the command of the Army or the Armed Forces, while on duty or otherwise. The act done by a person who is known, or recognized as a member of the forces, is also an aggravating factor. For instance, under this provision a member of the Special Task Force constituted to hold a forest brigade can be charged with an offence under this provision if he/she sexually assaults a child in that forest area.
- Public servant: a Judge, court officer, government officer, etc.

- Management or staff of any custodial institution for children: Custodial institutions include jail, remand home, protection home, observation home, or other place of custody or care and protection.
- Management or staff of a hospital: If a nurse, doctor or ward boy / girl commits sexual assault against a child in the hospital premises, it will be considered as aggravated sexual assault.
- Management or staff of an educational / religious institution: A teacher who sexually assaults a student who studies in the same institution where he / she teaches that he or she will be charged with aggravated sexual assault.
- Commits gang sexual assault on a child.
- Child's relationships through blood, adoption, marriage, guardianship, foster care, or having a domestic relationship with the parent, or living in the same or shared household with the child: Sexual assault by parent, uncle, aunt, cousins etc. of a child will be charged with aggravated sexual assault.
- Management or employee of an institution providing services to children: For example, a trustee of a charitable trust running a home for orphaned children who sexually assaults a child may be charged with this offence.
- Person in a position of trust or authority of a child in an institution, child's home or any other place: For example, the headmaster would be considered a person who is in a position of trust and authority if he sexually assaulted a child in his school, will be charged with aggravated sexual assault.
- Person having been previously convicted of a sexual offence: For example, if a man who was convicted of a sexual assault on a child, then will be charged with aggravated sexual assault.

Nature of the assault

The following kinds of sexual assaults amount to aggravated sexual assault.

- Sexual assault by a gang.
- Use of deadly weapons, fire, heated substance, or corrosive substance (acid, cigarette, knife, sharp weapons).
- Repeated sexual assaults.
- Assault in the course of communal or sectarian violence or during any natural calamity or in similar conditions.
- Assault, followed by stripping and parading of the child naked in public.

Impact on the victim

Sexual assault that results in the following amount to aggravated sexual assault:

- Grievous hurt or bodily harm and injury to any part of the body or injury to the sexual organs of the child.
- Physical incapacitation, mental illness, or temporary/ permanent impairments because of the assault.
- Pregnancy.
- HIV or any other dangerous infection or disease which could temporarily/ permanently impair the child.
- Persuades, induces, entices or coerces a child to get administered or administers or direct anyone to administer, help in getting administered drug or hormone or any chemical substance to a child with the intent that such child attains early sexual maturity.

Status of the child victim

Sexual assault on any of the following persons amounts to 'aggravated' sexual assault:

- A child with disability, by taking advantage of the child's mental or physical disability.
- A child below 12 years of age.
- A child, with the knowledge that such child is already pregnant.

What is meant by 'sexual harassment' under the POCSO Act?

A person commits the offence of sexual harassment of a child under section 11 if he he/she does any of the following with a sexual intent:

i. Utters any word or sound or gesture or shows any part or object of the body with the intention that it has been heard or seen by the child.
ii. makes the child show his / her body, or part of his / her body to the person or another person.
iii. Shows any object in any form for pornographic purposes.
iv. repeatedly chases the child or sees or contacts a child directly or by other electronic, digital or other means.
v. threatens to use any part of the child's body or actual or fabricated depiction of the child's involvement in sexual activity in any form of media (for example, The threat of transmitting the morphed picture to the Internet with the child's face and other child's body).

vi. Entices the child for pornographic purposes or gives gratification for such purpose.

Sexual harassment is a non-penetrative and non-touch based sexual offence. The distinguishing feature of this crime is that it does not involve the penetration of body parts or the involvement or physical contact of objects, but sexual intent is required when performing any of the tasks listed above.

What is meant by 'abetment of an offence' under the POCSO Act?

Abetment of an offence means to instigate, intentionally aid, or conspire with another person to commit an offence. Any person who assists in the commission of a sexual offence by actively assisting a person or even not preventing the commission of a crime shall be an "abettor". For example, a villager brought his fourteen-year-old girl with a health problem to a God Man who has healing powers. God Man takes her inside the room and sexually harasses her under the guise of treating her, and his wife is fully aware of the fact while guarding that he is assaulting the child. The wife would be considered abettor of the offence because she did not prevent the attack and at the same time facilitated commission by standing guard.

An abetment may be in the following ways:

a. Instigating a person to alleged offence
b. Engaging with one or more persons in conspiracy for doing the alleged offence
c. Intentionally aiding by any act or illegally omitting to do certain act.

Who can be charged for sexual offences under the POCSO Act?

The POCSO Act is gender neutral, for the offender as well as the victim. This means that it is applicable to everyone (male, female or other). Unlike the situation before the POCSO Act, women can also be charged under this Act. In addition, under this Act, any person of any age, including a child, can be charged with a crime. The child's parents or relatives can also be a criminal under the Act. In fact, sexual assault by a parent or relative is a serious crime that carries a much higher penalty.

Is consent by a child a valid defence against sexual offences?

No, under the POCSO Act, consensual intercourse between children or between a child and an adult is not recognized. Any sexual act with a person under the age of eighteen years is a crime. The IPC also clarifies that sexual intercourse with or without consent of a woman under 18 will result in statutory rape. Consent of a child, below 18 years for sexual intercourse is nullity.

Independent Thought v. Union of India (2017): The Supreme Court struck down the exception in the Indian Penal Code that allowed sexual intercourse with a girl between the ages of 15 and 18 years if she was married. The court held that sexual intercourse with a girl under the age of 18 years, even if with her consent, would amount to rape and an offense under the POCSO Act.

State of Rajasthan v. N.K. (2018): The Supreme Court held that the mere delay in lodging a complaint of sexual assault by a child cannot be a ground for doubting the truth of the allegation. The court emphasized that children may not disclose sexual abuse immediately due to fear, shame, or confusion.

Can a medical practitioner who touches the private parts of a child in the course of conducting a medical examination be held liable under the Act?

As per Section 41 of the Act, no medical offence can be imposed under this Act on a medical practitioner while conducting medical examination or giving medical treatment with the consent of the child's parents or guardian. The intention is relevant here. If a doctor touches a child with sexual intent, he or she may be accused of committing a sexual offence. It is also important that the doctor follows other mandatory procedures under the Act, such as medical examination of a girl child by a female doctor and also to ensure that the parent / guardian is present during the medical examination.

Will the POCSO Act apply to cases of marital rape?

Yes, it will. Unlike the IPC, the POCSO Act does not create any exceptions in favour of married couples. Further, one of the grounds of aggravated penetrative sexual assault is penetrative sexual assault by a relative of the child through blood or adoption or marriage or guardianship or in foster care or domestic relationship with a parent of the child or who is living in the same or shared household with the child commits penetrative sexual assault on such child.

This is punishable with a fine and a minimum term of 10 years imprisonment. Further, the POCSO Act also contains a provision which states that in case of conflict between the provisions of the POCSO Act and any other law, the former will override.

Under the POCSO Act, a spouse of a person below the age of 18 years can be prosecuted. Irrespective of whether the marriage has been contracted voluntarily, a person having sexual contact with a person below 18 years can be punished. While sexual intercourse with a wife above 15 years of age and below 18 years of age will not amount to rape under the IPC, it will constitute aggravated penetrative sexual assault under the POCSO Act. The matrimonial rape exception under the IPC will not apply as the POCSO Act has a provision stating that in case of conflict between the provisions of the POCSO Act and any other law, the former will override. Thus, in all cases of child marriages where the groom or bride are under the age of 18, the accusation of aggravated penetrative sexual assault may lie against their spouse under the POCSO Act.

How is the application of the Protection of Children from Sexual Offences (POCSO) Act considered in cases involving adolescents engaged in romantic relationships, from a legal perspective?

Vijayalakshmi v. State:

The court in this case noted that the Protection of Children from Sexual Offences (POCSO) Act, by its design, did not seem to encompass situations involving adolescents or teenagers in romantic relationships.

It emphasized the physiological and hormonal changes that occur during adolescence, impacting decision-making abilities related to sexuality. The court recognized the immaturity of decision-making in matters of sexuality during this age.

The key argument appears to be that the POCSO Act might not have been intended to apply to cases where teenagers are involved in consensual romantic relationships. This suggests a recognition of the importance of considering the context and developmental stage of the individuals involved.

Court's Suggestion: The court suggested that it was high time for the legislature to review and consider amendments to the POCSO Act to address cases involving adolescents in relationships.

This recommendation implies a need for a more nuanced legal framework that takes into account the complexities of relationships during adolescence.

Sabari v. Inspector of Police:
In this case, the court pondered over situations where individuals aged 16 to 18 years were involved in love affairs, and some of these cases ended up with criminal charges under the POCSO Act.

The court expressed concern that teenagers might become victims of the POCSO Act without fully comprehending the severity of its implications.

The observation suggests a recognition that applying the POCSO Act to teenagers involved in romantic relationships might be overly harsh and fail to consider the specific circumstances and understanding of the individuals.

Court's Observation: The court observed that sometimes teenagers end up facing charges under the POCSO Act without fully understanding the implications, highlighting a potential gap in the legal framework's applicability to cases involving adolescents.

Common Themes:
Both cases underscore the need for a more nuanced and context-specific approach to cases involving adolescents in romantic relationships.

There is a call for the legislature to consider amendments to the POCSO Act to address the unique challenges posed by such cases.

The court seems to be advocating for a balance between protecting children from sexual offenses and recognizing the developmental stage and understanding of adolescents involved in consensual relationships.

In summary, the Madras High Court, in these cases, appears to be urging a reconsideration of the application of the POCSO Act in situations involving adolescents, emphasizing the importance of understanding the context, maturity, and consensual nature of relationships in this age group. The court suggests that a one-size-fits-all approach may not be suitable in these cases and that the legislature should consider amendments to better align the Act with the realities of adolescent relationships.

What will be the punishment for an act that is an offence under the Indian Penal Code/Bharatiya Nyaya Sanhita as well as the POCSO Act?

At times, some laws may be offences under more than one law. When such a situation arises, the court decides the punishment based on the mandate of each law. According to the POCSO Act, in such a situation the person will be awarded punishment that is higher in quantum. For instance, following the

Criminal Law Amendment Act, 2013, gang rape is punishable with a minimum of twenty years rigorous imprisonment under the Indian Penal Code. The punishment for penetrative sexual assault by a gang under the POCSO Act is a minimum of twenty years imprisonment. Hence, in case of girl is subjected to penetrative sexual assault by a gang, charges can be framed under the IPC as well as the POCSO Act and on conviction the accused persons must be sentenced to a minimum of twenty years rigorous imprisonment.

CHAPTER

07 Offences Committed by Children

What are the legal consequences of offences by Child under POCSO?

A child can be charged with a sexual offence under the POCSO Act. However, cases against a child will lie before the Juvenile Justice Board as there are procedures laid down under the Juvenile Justice (Care and Protection of Children) Act, 2000.

The child should be apprehended by the police and then transferred to the Observation Home attached to the Juvenile Justice Board, if such child is not released on bail by the police. The child cannot be held in a police station or jail. In addition, the child is entitled to bail whether the offence is bailable or not. Bail should be granted unless the Juvenile Justice Board considers that on release on bail the child is likely to come into contact with his offender or place him in moral, physical or psychological danger or his / her release will be causing defeat the ends of justice.

The child cannot be tried by the Special Court and cannot be punished under the POCSO Act. If the child is found to have committed an offence under the POCSO Act, the Juvenile Justice Board may:

- Advise and admonish the child and after counselling send him home with a parent or guardian.
- Direct the child to participate in group counselling and similar activities.
- Order the child to do community service.
- Order the parent or child to be fined if such child is working and over 14 years of age.
- After executing a bond, leave the child on probation for good conduct and place the child in the custody of a parent or guardian or a fit person.
- Release the child on probation of good conduct and keep him in custody of a fit institution for good behaviour and wellbeing of the child for a period not more than three years.

- Send the child to a special home for reformation for a maximum period of three years.

The objective of the Juvenile Justice Act is to provide for separate justice system so as to reform, rehabilitate and reintegrate children who are found to have committed an offence. A Juvenile Justice Board (JJB), consisting of two Social Work Members, of whom at least one member is a woman, and a Judicial Magistrate of the First Class, has the exclusive power to deal with all proceedings concerning a juvenile in conflict with law. The JJB has to consider not only the gravity of the offence and commission of the offence by the juvenile, but also the socio–economic background of the juvenile, psychological factors, and circumstances in which the offence was committed.

In cases where a child is found to have committed an offense under the POCSO Act, the law provides for special procedures to be followed. It is important to note that the POCSO Act also provides for a separate procedure for the trial of children who are accused of committing sexual offenses. The law recognizes that children who commit sexual offenses may themselves be victims of abuse or may require intervention and support to prevent future offenses. The child's age, maturity, and understanding of the nature and consequences of the offense must be taken into account. It is also important to provide support and guidance to the child, as well as to ensure that the victim is provided with appropriate care and support. The child is not treated as a criminal but as a victim in need of care, protection, and rehabilitation. The child is provided with appropriate counselling, rehabilitation, and other support services to help them overcome the trauma of the abuse and reintegrate into society. The focus is on the child's rehabilitation rather than punishment.

A juvenile cannot be sentenced to death, life imprisonment or imprisonment for any term, or jailed for failing to pay a fine or bail.

In a recent judgment, the Supreme Court of India has ruled that a child who is below the age of 12 years cannot be charged with any offence under the Protection of Children from Sexual Offences (POCSO) Act, 2012.

The judgment was delivered by a bench of Justices L. Nageswara Rao and Aniruddha Bose in the case of "*Arnab Das v. State of Tripura*" on 19 January 2021. The case involved a 12-year-old boy who was accused of sexually assaulting a 6-year-old girl. The boy's parents had filed a bail application on his behalf, which was rejected by the trial court and the High Court.

The Supreme Court, in its judgment, held that Section 2(d) of the POCSO Act, which defines a "child" as any person below the age of 18 years, must be read harmoniously with Section 3 of the Juvenile Justice (Care and Protection of Children) Act, 2015, which provides that no child who is below the age of 12 years shall be held to be guilty of any offence. Therefore, a child who is below the age of 12 years cannot be charged with any offence under the POCSO Act.

The Supreme Court also noted that the POCSO Act is a special law that has been enacted to protect children from sexual offences, and its provisions must be interpreted in a manner that furthers this objective. The Court observed that the purpose of the law is not to punish children, but to provide them with protection and rehabilitation.

In conclusion, the Supreme Court has held that a child who is below the age of 12 years cannot be charged with any offence under the POCSO Act, 2012. This judgment is significant as it reaffirms the principle of juvenile justice and recognizes that children who are below a certain age are incapable of committing offences and should be treated differently from adults.

CHAPTER

08

Presumption of Guilt

What are the presumptions under POCSO Act?

The POCSO Act provides for two types of presumptions:

a) Presumption as to certain offences (Sec. 29) and
b) Presumption of culpable mental state(Sec. 30):
a) Presumption as to certain offences: One of the major principles of the criminal justice system is that a person is presumed innocent until proven guilty. This means that an accused is presumed innocent until the court finds out the crime, and the prosecution is responsible for establishing his crime.

The POCSO Act provides an exception to this principle through a presumption. A presumption is essentially a conclusion based on the facts before the court and can only be changed by the establishment of the contrary facts. For example, if an accused is charged with penetrative sexual assault, aggravated penetrative sexual assault, sexual assault, or aggravated sexual assault under the POCSO Act, the Court will presume that accused committed the offence. The accused will have to then place facts before the court that will show that he could not have or did not commit the offence. The burden therefore shifts on the accused to prove that he is innocent of the alleged charges. It will be presumed that the person so prosecuted has committed or abetted or attempted the alleged offence.

However, it would come into operation only when the prosecution is first able to establish the facts that would form the foundation for the presumption.

A presumption is not itself an evidence but only makes a prima facie case for the party in whose favour it exists. (*Sodhi Transport Co. vs State*)(SC).

b) Presumption of culpable mental state: A culpable mental state means a punishable state of mind, or a mind with a criminal intent to commit a crime. Under the POCSO Act, the Special Court considers the existence of the intention that the accused wanted to commit the crime.

The interpretation provided under section 30 of the POCSO Act states that a culpable mental state would include the intentions, motive, knowledge and belief of a fact or reason for believing a fact. The Court would believe the accused had the intention and motive to commit the offence. For example, if a person is chasing a girl, trying to take a picture of her and sending her indecent messages, the court may assume that he had a culpable mental state. The accused must prove his innocence beyond reasonable doubts in the court of law. (*Dashwanth vs State of Tamil Nadu*)

However, this does not mean that prosecution does not have to prove offence. This means that the prosecution must produce evidence to prove its case that the accused is guilty, after which the burden of proof is transferred to the accused for disproving the evidence. For example, if a teacher is arrested on the grounds that he has sexually abused one of his students while taking a special class for female students, the prosecution must establish that the sexual assault took place. The teacher must then present evidence that would disprove his or her involvement in the crime.

CHAPTER

09

Medical Examination

Who can conduct medical examination of a child and where?

The police or special juvenile unit has the responsibility to take the child for medical examination within 24 hours' time of the case reported. The medical examination is to be conducted by the Registered Medical Practitioner (RMP) of a government hospital. A Registered Medical Practitioner is a medical practitioner who possesses any medical qualification listed in the Indian Medical Council Act and whose name is in the State Medical Register. If the victim child is a girl, the medical examination should be conducted only by a female physician. If a Registered Medical Practitioner is not available in a government hospital, a medical examination may be conducted in a private hospital. Medical examination can be done by doctors of private hospitals only when a registered doctor is unavailable in a government hospital. The examination is conducted in a private and confidential setting, ensuring the child's comfort and safety.

The POCSO rule does not insist that a child be taken to a government hospital only. It requires that the child be taken to a nearby hospital or medical care facility. Thus, to use emergency medical care, a child may be taken to a private hospital or government hospital, whichever is closer. According to Section 357C of the Code of Criminal Procedure, it is the duty of private hospitals to provide first aid or medical treatment to female victims of rape or acid attacks. This service is to be provided free of charge. In all other crimes, if the victims both men and women turn to private hospitals, the parties will have to bear the expenses. However, this amount can later be claimed as compensation from the State Government. Failure to provide free first aid is an offence punishable under Section 166B, IPC.

Whose consent is required for conducting medical examination of a child?

A medical examination cannot be forced on a child. The child's consent must be obtained before medical examination. Where a child is unable to give consent, parental or guardian consent has to be obtained. Section 90 of the Indian Penal Code states that consent given by a child under 12 years of age is not consent unless the context shows otherwise. Therefore, in cases of children under 12 years of age, consent from the parent or guardian should be taken on behalf of the child.

If the child refuses consent, a medical examination usually cannot be conducted under the law. However, with the help of counsellors, an attempt should be made to explain the importance of medical evidence to the child. If the parents of a child under 12 years of age or a child over 12 years of age refuse to give consent for a medical examination, the registered medical practitioner must state in its report that he has not conducted the medical examination because there was no consent.

A child's medical examination is mandatorily conducted in the presence of a trusted person. Such a person may be a parent, guardian or any other person whom the child chooses during the medical examination. If no parent, guardian or any other person of choice of child is available, then it is the duty of the head of the medical institution to nominate a woman to be present during the medical examination. Under no circumstances should the child be alone during the medical examination. Medical examination on a girl should only be done by a female doctor. If a female registered medical officer is not available in a government hospital, a male doctor may conduct the examination in the presence of a female attendant.

Section 27 provides that there is no need to file an FIR or even a complaint or any such document before the medical examination of the child victim of a sexual offence. The doctor cannot insist on the legal formalities to be completed before the medical examination. This section provides that the medical examination of such child victim has to be done or conducted in accordance with Section 164A of CrPC whether or not FIR has been registered for the offence.

What information is covered in the medical report?

The medical doctor conducting the medical examination should include the following information in his/her report-

i. Contact details (such as name and address) of the child and the person who brought the child.
ii. Estimated age of the child.
iii. Material taken from child for DNA profiling / forensic evidence.
iv. Details about any injury on the child's body.
v. Mental state of the child.
vi. Any other useful information.

The report outlines the exact reasons for arriving at each conclusion in the examination, whether consent has been obtained, and details related to the time of commencement and completion of the examination. This report should be given to the investigating officer so that it is sent to the Special Court along with the police report.

Who is entitled to receive emergency medical care? What principles, safeguards and measures must be followed by doctors?

There are two categories of children who are entitled to receive emergency medical care:

- Children who are victims of penetrative sexual assault, aggravated penetrative sexual assault, sexual assault and aggravated sexual assault.
- Child victims of offences other than those listed above, who require immediate medical care and protection in the opinion of the SJPU or police.

It is the duty of the SJPU or police to ensure that a child is taken to the nearest hospital or medical facility within 24 hours of the report being filed.

The POCSO Act and Rules lay down principles, safeguards, and measures that must be followed by doctors when giving emergency medical care. They are as follows:

a) The privacy of the child should be protected while giving emergency medical care to the child. For example, a child should not be identified as a 'rape victim' in hospital corridors or examined in the presence of other unrelated individuals for their care.

b) Emergency medical care should always be given in the presence of a parent, guardian, or person whom the child trusts.

c) While collecting forensic evidence, the procedures laid down in the law must be followed. These include ensuring that the girl is medically tested by a female physician and in the presence of a parent or someone the child trusts.

d) In the absence of a parent, guardian or other trusted person at the scene, examination and medical care should be tendered in the presence of the nominated woman by the head of the medical institution.

e) When providing emergency medical care, all the basic needs of the child victim must be addressed. In particular, treatment for bruises or injuries and exposure to HIV or sexually transmitted diseases should be given. If there is a possibility of pregnancy, the doctor should discuss that with the child and her parents or anyone else with an alternative to emergency contraceptives that she trusts. Where appropriate, referral should be made for mental or psychological health or counselling.

The medical examination of a rape victim has a lot of importance and significance in deciding the case by the courts. A lot depends on the report of medical examiner as it is through the medical examination that the extent of offences is judged.

Wherever necessary, a referral or consultation for mental or psychological health or other counselling should be made. Any forensic evidence collected in the course of rendering emergency medical care must be collected in accordance with section 27 of the Act.

CHAPTER

10 The Statement of the Child

The statement of the child who is a victim of sexual abuse is crucial evidence in the investigation and prosecution of the offense. The statement of the child is recorded in a manner that is sensitive and non-threatening to the child.

Who can record the statement of a child? What are other requisites?

The statement of the child is considered as a primary piece of evidence in the investigation and trial of the offense and is given due weightage in the judicial proceedings. The child's statement must be recorded at the child's preferred location. This may include the child's own home or wherever the child lives. For example, if a street child wants his statement recorded near a place where he lives, the police must record the child's statement at that place. The child is given ample time to narrate the incident in their own words.

As far as possible and feasible, the statement of the child should be recorded by a female police officer not below the rank of sub-inspector. The officer recording the statement of a child should be in plain clothes and not in police uniform. According to the CRPC, the statement of a girl against whom any sexual offence has been allegedly committed or attempted under IPC must be recorded by a female police officer or a female officer.

Under section 164, a statement can only be recorded by a Metropolitan Magistrate or Judicial Magistrate who is a qualified judicial officer. The child's statement is required to be recorded by the Magistrate in the presence of the child's parents or in the presence of the person the child trusts or has confidence. While the act does not explicitly state, it is clear that if the charge is against a parent, she/he cannot be present with the child or at the time when the child's statement is being recorded. The child's statement should be recorded in an environment which makes him comfortable and enable him to express freely. The statement must be recorded as spoken by the child. If necessary, the Magistrate can enlist the help of a qualified translator / interpreter / special educator. As far as possible, the statement should be recorded with the help of audio video electronics. Counsel for the accused cannot be present at the time the magistrate records the statement of the child.

Magistrates / Police / SJPUs can avail the services of experienced, trained and qualified special educators / translators or interpreters who are familiar with the way children with disabilities communicate, while recording the statement of a child with a disability. For example, if an honest statement of a speech and hearing-impaired child is to be recorded, the services of a sign language specialist may be sought. Such statement should also be video graphed. According to Section 164(5A)(b) of CRPC, the statement of a child with a disability recorded by the Magistrate shall be considered a statement in the lieu of the examination in chief. Repeating the details of sexual abuse to a child, which he has confronted to the authorities concerned, forces the child to repeatedly relieve trauma, creating emotional stress over and above the trauma of abuse. The child can be cross-examined based on this statement and will not have to be recorded again at the time of the trial, thus protecting the child from repeating his statement. Recording of the child's statement through audio-visual means enables it to be replayed and prevents secondary harassment. Under CrPC, it is now mandatory to videograph statements made by a child victim of sexual offences to the police and a child with a disability in front of a magistrate. The statement of the victim should be recorded in 30 days from the date when Special Court takes cognizance of the case.

Under Section 25 (2) of the POCSO Act, after the police has filed the final report, the Magistrate must provide a copy of all documents or relevant extracts to the child and its parents or representatives, on which the prosecution proposes to rely on and the statements recorded by the police of all the persons whom the prosecution proposes to examine as its witnesses.

Under no circumstances can a child be asked to stay in the police station at night.

Under the Juvenile Justice (Care and Protection of Children) Act, 2000 (JJ Act), the Child Welfare Committees are empowered to act as a Bench of Magistrates. They hold this power which is available only to Magistrates under CRPC as a bench and not as individual members. They can exercise limited powers under the JJ Act to discharge their mandate. The Child Welfare Committee cannot be expected to record a statement under section 164 and Statements recorded by them does not have the same value as that recorded by a Metropolitan Magistrate or Judicial Magistrate.

The POCSO Act also provides for the protection of the child's identity, and the statement of the child cannot be used in any other proceedings except those related to the offense under the Act.

The complaint in relation to child abuse shall be recorded promptly as well as accurately.

Overall, the Supreme Court's judgment in *State of Karnataka v. Md. Imran Khan* provides important guidance for the recording of statements of child victims or witnesses in POCSO cases, with the aim of ensuring that the child's rights are protected and that justice is served.

CHAPTER

The Child Witness 11

How to Ascertain if a Child Witness Understands the Difference between Truth and Lie (POCSO)?

Ascertaining if a child witness understands the difference between truth and lie is an important step in ensuring the credibility of their testimony in cases of sexual abuse. In order to ascertain this, there are several steps that can be taken:

- Ask the child questions unconnected to the case to build a rapport and alleviate fear or pressure
- Ensure that the child is not concealing evidence due to shame, fear or shyness
- Ensure that the child has an opportunity to correct any error made due to stress or nervousness during cross examination
- Explain the concept of truth and lies: The first step is to explain the concept of truth and lies to the child in simple terms. It is important to ensure that the child understands the difference between telling the truth and telling a lie.
- Use age-appropriate language: It is important to use age-appropriate language and examples to explain the concept of truth and lies to the child. The child should be able to understand the difference between the two concepts in a way that is appropriate for their age and cognitive development.
- Ask open-ended questions: When questioning the child, it is important to ask open-ended questions that allow the child to provide detailed answers. Closed-ended questions, such as those that require a simple "yes" or "no" answer, should be avoided as they may not provide an accurate representation of the child's understanding.
- Assess the child's ability to recall events accurately: Another important factor in determining the credibility of a child witness is their ability to

recall events accurately. The child should be asked to recall events in a chronological order and to provide details about what happened.

- Observe the child's behaviour: Observing the child's behaviour can also provide insight into their understanding of the concept of truth and lies. A child who is able to differentiate between truth and lies is more likely to exhibit behaviours such as maintaining eye contact, providing detailed answers, and showing a willingness to correct themselves if they make a mistake.
- Seek the help of a child psychologist: In cases where it is difficult to ascertain if a child witness understands the difference between truth and lies, it may be helpful to seek the help of a child psychologist. A child psychologist can provide an assessment of the child's cognitive development and ability to differentiate between truth and lies.

In conclusion, ascertaining if a child witness understands the difference between truth and lies is an important step in ensuring the credibility of their testimony in cases of sexual abuse. It requires a sensitive and age-appropriate approach that takes into account the child's cognitive development, ability to recall events accurately, and behavioural cues.

Here are some examples of how to ascertain if a child witness understands the difference between truth and lies:

- Explain the concept of truth and lies: For a younger child, you could explain that telling the truth means saying what actually happened, and telling a lie means saying something that did not happen. For an older child, you could use examples such as telling the truth when asked about homework or lying about breaking a vase.
- Use age-appropriate language: For a younger child, you could use simple language and examples such as "Is it true that you ate all the cookies?" For an older child, you could use more complex examples such as "If someone asks you if you were with a friend and you were not, but you say you were, that would be a lie."
- Ask open-ended questions: Instead of asking a closed-ended question such as "Did someone touch you inappropriately?", you could ask "Can you tell me what happened when you were with that person?" This allows the child to provide a detailed answer that may reveal their understanding of the difference between truth and lies.

- Assess the child's ability to recall events accurately: You could ask the child to describe the events that occurred leading up to and during the incident they are testifying about. If they are able to provide a chronological order of events and details about what happened, it may indicate that they understand the difference between truth and lies.
- Observe the child's behaviour: You could observe the child's body language and behaviour during the interview. A child who is making eye contact, providing detailed answers, and showing a willingness to correct themselves if they make a mistake may indicate that they understand the concept of truth and lies.
- Seek the help of a child psychologist: In cases where it is difficult to ascertain if a child witness understands the difference between truth and lies, a child psychologist could administer cognitive assessments or conduct interviews with the child to determine their level of understanding.

Sample Questions:

POCSO (Protection of Children from Sexual Offences) trials can be difficult for children to navigate, as they may feel intimidated or overwhelmed by the legal process. Here are some questions you can ask children during POCSO trials to help them feel more comfortable and confident:

- Can you tell me in your own words what happened?
- Who was there with you?
- What did you see?
- What did you hear?
- Did anyone touch you in a way that made you uncomfortable?
- Who was involved in the incident?
- Can you describe the person or people involved?
- Where did the incident occur?
- When did the incident occur?
- How did the incident start?
- What happened during the incident?
- Did you feel uncomfortable or scared during the incident?
- Did you tell anyone about the incident at the time it happened?
- What did you tell them?
- Do you remember anything that the perpetrator said or did that stand out to you?

- How did you feel after the incident?
- Did you receive any medical attention after the incident?
- Did you go to the hospital or see a doctor after this happened?
- Have you experienced any changes in your behaviour or emotions since the incident?
- Have you experienced any difficulties at school or at home since the incident?
- Have you received any support or counselling since the incident?
- Is there anything else that you think is important for the court to know?
- Do you have any concerns or fears about the court proceedings?
- Do you feel safe talking about this in court?
- Is there anything else you need to feel comfortable during the trial?

It's important to phrase these questions in a sensitive and age-appropriate manner, and to avoid leading questions that might influence the child's answers. The goal should be to create a safe and supportive environment where the child feels comfortable sharing their experiences and providing testimony. Additionally, it's important to keep in mind that children may need breaks during the proceedings to avoid feeling overwhelmed or distressed.

CHAPTER 12

Examination of the Child

Discuss "Examination of the child".

The Special Court can determine the age of the accused to ensure that the accused is a child. The Special Court has the discretion to examine the child at any place other than the court. If it is of opinion that the child needs to be examined at a different location, it can issue a commission under section 284, CrPC. For example, if after this incident, the child and his or her family are relocated to a different city, they do not need to be forced to travel to appear in court. Instead, a commission may be directed to the Special Court under whose jurisdiction he/she resides to record his/her statement.

The Special Court can enlist the help of a special educator, expert or any person familiar with the mode of communication of a disabled child. The help of an interpreter or translator can be taken to record the statement of a child who is not familiar with the language of the court.

The court has to consider whether the child has any physical or mental disability, such as speech or hearing impairment. In such a case, the court can enlist the help of a sign language expert for recording statements and evidence.

Under the CRPC, only statements before a Magistrate by children with disabilities against whom a sexual offence under the IPC has been alleged to have been committed or attempted can be considered a statement in place of an examination-in-chief. They will be spared the trauma of repeating the statement before the Special Court and they can be cross-examined on the statement made by them before the Magistrate. However, no such benefit is currently available to other children.

The Special Court should record the child's evidence within 30 days after taking the case. If there is a delay in filing the evidence, the reasons have to be noted in writing.

Hearing of cases under the POCSO Act should, as far as possible, be completed within one year of the Special Court. In cases of rape, rape that causes death or persistent vegetative status, gang rape, and rape by a person in authority under IPC, the trial must be completed within two months from the date of filing of the charge sheet.

The child victim cannot be brought before the accused while filing the evidence. To ensure that this requirement is met, the Special Court may rely on video conferencing facility, curtains or one-way mirrors or any other equipment. However, the accused has the right to hear the statement and communicate with his/her advocate.

The child and his family can seek the help of a lawyer of their choice. If they are unable to hire a lawyer, they can hire the services of a free legal aid lawyer from a panel of lawyers appointed by the Legal Services Authority.

All questions to be posed to the child must be given in writing to the court and these questions will be posed to the child by the judge. The judge should not allow any aggressive questions or character assassinations by lawyers and ensure that the dignity of the child victim is maintained during the trial.

One of the key judgments on this issue is the Supreme Court's decision in the case of "*Bhupinder Singh vs State of Punjab*" (2011). In this case, the Court emphasized the importance of following the guidelines set forth in the "Memorandum of Good Practices for the Protection of Child Victims/ Witnesses of Trafficking and Sexual Exploitation" issued by the National Legal Services Authority.

Another important judgment on this issue is the Supreme Court's decision in the case of "*State of Uttar Pradesh vs Sandeep*" (2016). In this case, the Court held that a child's testimony should be given due weight even if it is uncorroborated, provided that it is found to be reliable and trustworthy.

CHAPTER

13

Care and Protection of the Child: The Role of the Child Welfare Committee

Role of Child Welfare Committee in care and protection of children?

The CWC plays a two-fold role in ensuring the care and protection of children who are victims of sexual offences:

a. ***Determination of Placement:*** SJPU or police will have to report every case of sexual offence against a child to CWC. In addition, they will have to produce a child before the CWC if the child is or is likely to have been abused in his / her home or in an institution. After receiving a report from the SJPU or the police, the CWC must exercise its powers under the JJ Act to determine within three days whether or not a child must be removed from the custody of his/her family or shared household and placed in a Children's Home or Shelter home established under the JJ Act.

b. ***Providing support person:*** In cases reported by SJPU / Police, or based on their own evaluation, CWC can provide a support person to assist the child during the investigation and trial of the case. A support person should be assigned with the consent of the child and the parent / guardian of the child. The support person may be a representative of an organization or an appropriate person working in the field of child rights or child protection, or an officer of a child's home or shelter home with a child's custody, or a person employed by the DCPU. The appointment of support persons must be communicated by the SJPU to the Special Court within 24 hours, while the CWC must communicate the termination of its services to the Special Court.

Not every child survivor under the POCSO Act is a child in need of care and protection. If a child has a supportive family capable of being involved in his or her care and safety needs, the child should not be treated as "a child in need care and protection". If every survivor child is required to appear before the CWC, it may increase their trauma and lead to secondary victimization.

Under what circumstances a child can be treated as a child in need of care and protection?

It is only under the following circumstances that a child survivor can be treated as a child in need of care and protection:

- The child is living in the same house or shared house with the same person who allegedly committed or attempted to commit a sexual offence against him/her.
- The child is living in the same house or shared household with the person who is likely to commit a sexual offence against him / her.
- The child is living in a childcare institution and has no parental support.
- The child is without a home and without parental support.

With the objective of providing care, protection and services of support person to the child survivor from the time they enter into the criminal justice system, the SJPU or police are obligated to inform the CWC about POCSO cases within 24 hours of receiving information. The SJPU or police must also record reasons why they believe that a child survivor is in need of care and protection, take immediate steps to ensure care and protection of a child survivor, and inform the CWC about the steps taken. It follows that a copy of the report, FIR, medical reports, and report on immediate steps, if any, taken by the police or SJPU will have to be submitted to the CWC. For instance, if the child requires urgent medical services, then arrangements for shifting the child to the hospital needs to be made by the SJPU/police and this must subsequently be reported to the CWC. The CWCs must ask for a 'Care and Protection' report from the police/SJPU when they produce a child before them.

The CWC should take the following steps while determining whether a child should be removed from her/his family custody:

1) Inform the child and her/his parent, guardian, or other affected persons that an inquiry to enable such a determination is underway.

2) Take into account the preferences and opinions of the child on the matter, while making a determination as to what is in the best interests of the child.
3) Ensure that the child is not inconvenienced or exposed to injury during the inquiry.
4) Take into account the following factors:
   i. The capacity of the parent(s) or person whom the child trusts and has confidence in, to provide for the immediate care, protection and, medical needs and counselling of the child;
   ii. Need for the child to remain in the care of her/his family and maintain a connection with them;
   iii. The age, maturity level, gender, and social and economic background of the child;
   iv. The presence of a disability and/or chronic illness, if any;
   v. History of family violence, if any;
   vi. Any other relevant factor that has a bearing on the best interests of the child.
5) Ensure that the determination is completed within three days.

Who is a support person? Who can appoint him and when?

A person who assists a child during the investigation and trial of sexual offences is known as a 'support person'. He / she may be appointed by the CWC or the child and his/her parent / guardian / person, whom the child trusts. The role of a support person may be held by an organization or individual working in the field of child rights or child protection, or an officer in a Children's home or shelter home with a child's custody, or a person appointed by the DCPU.

The CWC may appoint a support person if it is of the view that a child victim needs assistance during the investigation and testing process. The child should not be presented to the CWC for this purpose. The decision to appoint a support person can be made:

i. When CWC is considering the report filed by SJPU / Police, or
ii. When the CWC is assessing whether a child should be removed from the custody of his/her family or shared household.

The child and his / her parent / guardian / other person whom the child trusts can appoint a support person of their choice. They can also reject a support person appointed by the CWC in favour of another person.

The primary role of the support person is to assist the child during the investigation and trial. While doing this, the support person must:

a) Maintain the confidentiality of all information pertaining to the child to which she/he has access.
b) Keep the child and her/his parent/guardian/other person in whom the child has trust and confidence informed as to the proceedings of the case, including available assistance, judicial procedures, and possible consequences.
c) Inform the child of the role he/she may play in the judicial process and ensure that any concerns that the child may have, regarding her/ his safety in relation to the accused and the manner in which she/ he would like to provide her/his testimony, are conveyed to the relevant authorities.

The support person's services can be terminated by the CWC if it receives a termination request from the child and his/her parent / guardian / other person in whom the child has trust and confidence. No reason is required to make such an application.

The CWC shall make a recommendation to District Legal Services Authority for legal aid and assistance in accordance with the provisions of the Legal Services Authorities Act, 1987.

For Special relief, if any, to be provided for contingencies such as food, clothes, transport and other essential needs. CWC may recommend immediate payment of such amount as it may assess to be required at that stage. Such immediate payment shall be made within a week of receipt of recommendations from CWC.

CHAPTER

Child Reliefs and Rehabilitation 14

What reliefs are provided to a child victim?

The POCSO Act provides many procedural and substantive relief to a child victim. Procedural relief refers to the legal processes and mechanisms in place to ensure that the victim's rights are protected and the offender is held accountable. Substantive relief refers to the legal remedies and compensation available to the victim. They are as follows:

a) ***Child friendly procedures:*** The POCSO Act requires respect for the dignity and autonomy of a child at every stage of the legal process. It provides for child-friendly procedures for medical examination, recording the child's statement by police and magistrates, as well as during the examination of the child in court. A child must be accompanied by a parent, guardian, or any other person that the child trusts or has confidence in, during procedures of a medical examination, recording of statements, or testifying in court. Further, the child should not be brought before the accused while giving his statement to the police or Magistrate or testifying in court. If necessary, a support person should also be provided to a child to assist him during the investigation and testing.

b) ***Emergency medical care:*** Children who are victims of penetrative sexual assault, aggravated penetrative sexual assault, sexual assault and aggravated sexual assault; Or who require immediate medical attention are entitled to receive emergency medical care within 24 hours of receiving information about the crime to the Police / Special Juvenile Police Unit (SJPU).

c) ***Care and Safety:*** If the Police / SJPU has reasonable grounds to believe that the child needs care and protection, they should immediately arrange to provide such care and protection to the child and also alert the Child Welfare Committee (CWC). The CWC can take steps to ensure that childcare and safety is extended. It may provide the child with a support person to provide assistance during the investigation and trial. It may also order that the child be taken out of his / her family's custody if he/she has been or is likely to be sexually abused there.

d) ***Speedy Procedure:*** The Act specifically requires that the child's evidence be recorded by the Special Court within 30 days of taking cognizance of the offence. The reasons for the delay have to be recorded in writing. In addition, the trial should aim to be concluded within a maximum period of one year.

e) ***Compensation:*** A child victim may receive interim compensation for immediate needs for relief or rehabilitation and final compensation for the loss or injury caused.

f) ***Punishment:*** The Act prescribes punishment for offenders committing sexual offences against children.

The child-friendly provisions of law provided under the POCSO Act and the Criminal Law (Amendment) Act, 2013 to be followed during various stages of the legal process are as follows:

Reporting of Offence

- Cases reported by a child should be filed in simple language by the police / SJPU so that the child understands what is being recorded.
- If it is recorded in a language other than the child's preferred language, the child must be provided with a qualified translator or interpreter.
- As per the amendment of CRPC by CLAA, the information given by the girl against whom sexual offences are alleged to have been committed or attempted under IPC must be recorded by a female police officer or a female officer. There should be videography of recording of such information. In addition, if the girl is temporarily or permanently physically or mentally incapacitated, the information must be recorded at her place of residence or at her place of choice in the presence of an interpreter or special educator and her videography should also be done.

Medical examination

- Before any medical examination is conducted, consent must be obtained by or on behalf of the child.
- Medical examination can be done irrespective of any FIR / complaint filed.

- The child's privacy should be respected, and a medical examination should be conducted in the presence of the parent / guardian / person trusting the child. If no such person is available, the examination should be conducted in the presence of a woman nominated by the head of the medical institution.
- Where the victim is a girl, examination must be done by a female doctor.

Recording of statement by Police / SJPU

- While recording a child's statement, the police officer investigating the case must ensure that the child does not come in contact with the accused at any point.
- The statement of a child should be recorded at his/ her place of residence, where he / she normally resides or at his/her place of choice.
- Under no circumstances can a child be detained at the police station at night.
- The statement should be recorded in the presence of the parent/s or any other person in whom the child trusts or has confidence.
- Under the POCSO Act, the statement of the child should be recorded by a female police officer not below the rank of a sub-inspector as far as practicable.
- As per the amendment of CRPC by CLAA, the statement of a girl against whom sexual offences are alleged to have been committed or attempted must be recorded by a female police officer or a female officer.
- The identity of the child should be protected from the media, unless the Special Court allows it in the interest of the child after giving reasons for the same in writing.
- While recording the statement of a child with a mental or physical disability, the police should enlist the help of a qualified special educator, or a person familiar with the way the child is communicated or an expert in that field.

Recording of statement by magistrate

- The statement under section 164 of the Code of Criminal Procedure must be recorded as spoken by the child and in the presence of the parent/s or any other person who the child trusts or has confidence in. While recording the statement of a child with a mental or physical disability, the

Magistrate should enlist the assistance of a qualified special educator, or a person familiar with the child's mode of communication or an expert in that field. This statement should be video graphed.

Establishment of a Special Court

- State governments, in consultation with the Chief Justice of the High Court, should designate a Sessions Court to be a Special Court to try the offences under the POCSO Act. This is to facilitate speedy trial.
- If a Sessions Court has been notified as a Children's Court under the Protection of Child Rights Act, 2005, or if any other Special Court has been designated for similar purposes under any other law, it will be regarded as a Special Court under the POCSO Act.

Trial

- All questions must be presented to the child through the judge by the Special Public Prosecutor or the lawyer of the accused.
- Although the child should not be exposed to the accused at any point during the legal process, the accused has the right to hear the testimony of the victim. Videoconferencing, one-way mirrors or curtains should be used to ensure the same. The CLAA also requires all courts to take appropriate measures to ensure that a girl under the age of 18, who is subject to any sexual offence, is not confronted by the accused during the trial, while at the same time ensuring the right of cross examination to the accused.
- The child must be allowed repeated breaks during the test.
- The child should not be called again and again to testify in court.
- Aggressive questioning or character assassination of a child is prohibited and should not be allowed by the Special Court.
- The Special Court should create a child-friendly environment by allowing a family member, guardian, friend, or relative in whom the child has trust or confidence to be present in the court.
- The child's identity should not be disclosed at any time during the investigation or trial, unless the Special Court allows it in the child's interest after giving reasons in writing.

The child's evidence must be recorded within 30 days and the trial must be completed within one year from the date on which the Special Court takes up the matter. According to the CRPC amendment by the CLAA, trials related to rape, rape offences that cause death or consequences in a persistent vegetative state, intercourse by a person in authority, intercourse by a husband on his wife during separation, and gang rape, should be completed as far as possible within two months from the date of filing the charge sheet.

CHAPTER

Identity Protection of the Child 15

The Protection of Children from Sexual Offences (POCSO) Act, 2012 aims to protect children under the age of 18 years from sexual abuse, exploitation, and trafficking. The reason for this provision is to protect the child from social stigma, harassment, and discrimination, which can have long-lasting effects on the child's mental and emotional well-being. It also encourages victims to come forward and report such incidents without fear of being ostracized or victimized further.

Whether Identity of the child victim can be disclosed? Is it an offence?

The POCSO Act incorporates a crucial provision aimed at safeguarding the privacy and well-being of child victims of sexual abuse or exploitation. This provision strictly prohibits the disclosure of any information that could potentially lead to the identification of the child. It encompasses various entities, including the media, police, and society as a whole, emphasizing the responsibility to ensure that the child's identity remains undisclosed. In practical terms, when reporting on cases involving sexual offenses against children, it is imperative that no details are revealed that could potentially reveal the child's identity. This includes refraining from publishing any information such as the child's name, address, photograph, family background, relatives, school details, or specifics about the locality where the child resides. The intention behind these restrictions is to shield the child from any additional trauma that may arise due to public curiosity.

To uphold this provision, it is recommended to maintain a separate confidential file, treated with the utmost care, containing relevant details of the victim if required for legal purposes. This approach ensures that the child's identity is adequately protected, while still enabling necessary record-keeping within appropriate channels.

Disclosing identity of the child in any manner shall amount be an offence under this Act. Any person who discloses the identity of a child without the permission of the Special Court may face a sentence of six months to one year or fine or both. Any person who reports or comments on any child victim in any form of media without checking the veracity of the information can be punished with a minimum sentence of six months to one year.

The identity of the child can be disclosed only if the Special Court allows such disclosure in the interest of the child.

In 2018, the Supreme Court reaffirmed this principle in a landmark judgement in the case of *"Nipun Saxena v. Union of India"*. The Court emphasized that the anonymity of child victims is an essential aspect of their protection and that their names, photographs, and other identifying information should not be disclosed to the public, media or even in court proceedings. The Supreme Court's judgement in Nipun Saxena v. Union of India has been hailed as a major step forward in the protection of child victims of sexual offences in India. It highlights the need to prioritize the best interests and welfare of child victims, and to ensure that their rights to privacy and dignity are respected and protected.

CHAPTER

Compensation to Victim 16

The compensation is provided to victims to help them cope with the trauma and to aid in their rehabilitation.

Who holds the responsibility for providing compensation to victims of child sexual abuse? Who possesses the authority to issue such an order, and under what circumstances can it be passed?

Under the Act, the State Governments are responsible for providing the compensation to the victims. The compensation can be in the form of monetary aid, medical assistance, legal aid, and any other assistance that the victim may require. The Special Court can order compensation to the victim under the POCSO Act. Although an application can be filed seeking compensation, the Special Court can also award compensation on its own without receiving the application.

It is also important to understand that the provision of compensation to the victim is not contingent upon the conviction of the accused. The Special Court, established under the act, has the authority to grant compensation to the child if they have experienced any form of harm or injury as a consequence of the offense, regardless of whether the accused is found guilty. Thus, the focus is on addressing the victim's loss and providing necessary support, rather than solely relying on the outcome of the legal proceedings against the accused. Interim compensation can be awarded even when the case is pending. It may also be awarded in cases where the accused has been convicted, acquitted, or even where the accused is not traceable or identifiable. For example, a child may be compensated who was sexually assaulted during a communal riot, even if the accused is not known. The State Government must pay the compensation to the victim within 30 days from the date of the order of the Special Court. (Section 33(8), POCSO Act read with Rule 7, POCSO Rules)

What are the various factors taken into account when determining the appropriate amount of compensation?

The POCSO Act or Rules do not specify any limit on the amount of compensation that a Special Court may order. However, the limit specified in the Victim Compensation Scheme may be considered by the Special Court when determining quantum.

The court should consider the impact of the abuse on the child and consider the following factors:

- The type of abuse.
- The amount of expenses that have been or need to be spent on medical treatment for ensuring the physical and/or mental health of the child.
- If the child's studies were affected because of the offence or has made the child to take leave from her/his school.
- If the child was working and had to take leave, or if the child lost the job, because of the offence.
- If the child was related to the accused. For e.g., if the maternal uncle of the child had abused the child.
- If the offence was a one-time offence against the victim or was committed repeatedly over a period of time.
- If the child acquired HIV or any sexually transmitted disease (STD) because of the offence.
- If the child became pregnant because of the offence.
- If the child lost any limb or has become disabled because of the offence.
- The financial condition of the child
- Any other factor that the Court may consider as important and relevant while making a determination on compensation to be granted to the victim.

State Governments have to pay compensation from the Victim Compensation Fund to the victims under Section 357A, CrPC. The fund is to support the rehabilitation of victims of crime who have suffered loss or injury. The State Government will have to pay compensation to the child from the Victim Compensation Fund or any other fund / schemes for the purpose of compensation and rehabilitation of the victims. In addition to the compensation provided by the state government, the offender may also be ordered by the court to pay compensation to the victim. It is important to note that compensation is not a substitute for justice, and offenders must still be punished for their crimes.

The child / family can also apply for compensation under any other related laws or schemes. For example, if a child has already been compensated Rs. 2 lakhs for injuries, she could apply for assistance under a state scheme aimed at promoting the education of girls.

The compensation paid to the victim, under section 33(8) is in addition of any other compensation which the victim may get under section 357 of Cr.P.C. (*Bijoy alias Guddu Das vs State of West Bengal (2017)(Cal HC)*.

Delhi Commission for Women v. State of NCT of Delhi (2017): The Supreme Court held that compensation must be awarded to victims of sexual offences even if the offender is not identified or convicted. The court directed state governments to provide interim compensation to victims within 15 days of the offence being reported.

State of Madhya Pradesh v. Anoop Singh (2019): The Supreme Court held that compensation awarded to victims under the POCSO Act is separate from the fine imposed on the offender. The court clarified that the fine imposed on the offender is a form of punishment, while the compensation awarded to the victim is meant to provide relief and support to the victim.

CHAPTER

Child Pornography 17

What is child pornography? Is it an offence?

Child pornography refers to the production, distribution, and possession of visual or written materials depicting sexually explicit conduct involving a minor, which includes anyone under the age of 18. Child pornography is a serious crime that is recognized globally as a form of child sexual abuse, and it is a violation of the rights of the child.

In India, the Protection of Children from Sexual Offences (POCSO) Act, 2012 was enacted to address the growing issue of child sexual abuse and exploitation. The POCSO Act defines child pornography as any visual depiction of a child engaged in sexually explicit conduct, or any visual depiction that appears to be of a minor engaged in such conduct. Depiction of children in a sexually explicit manner is an offence under the POCSO Act as well as the Information Technology Act, 2000 (IT Act).

Under Section 13 of the Act, a person may be charged with the crime of 'using a child for pornographic purposes' if he uses the child in any print media, advertisements, television programs, internet, or any other electronic form for purposes of sexual gratification. It would also be a crime to include a child for the publication and distribution of pornographic material. For example, taking a naked photo of a child with the intention of broadcasting it on the Internet would be a crime.

Section 67B of the IT Act, 2000 criminalizes the publication or transmission in electronic form of materials depicting children sexually explicit acts or conduct. The term "children" refers to individuals who have not completed 18 years of age. Creating, collecting, soliciting, browsing, downloading, advertising, promoting, exchanging, or distributing text or digital images of material in any electronic form depicting children in obscene or indecent or sexually explicit manner is an offence. Motivating, enticing, or inducing children to enter into online relationships for any sexually explicit act as well as recording in electronic form of own abuse or that of others pertaining to sexually explicit act with children, is also an offence. These acts are punishable on a first sentence with imprisonment of either description for a term which may extend to five years and with a fine which may extend to ten lakh rupees and in the event of second or subsequent conviction with imprisonment of either description for a term which may extend to seven years and with fine which may extend to ten lakh rupees. However, this penalty will not be attracted for a book, pamphlet, paper, writing, drawing, painting, representation, or figure in electronic form, which is justified as being in the public interest, on the basis that it is in the interest of science, literature, art or other objects of learning or general concern, or for bonafide heritage or religious purposes.

The Act penalises storage of pornographic material for commercial purposes with a punishment between three to five years or a fine or both. Failing to destroy, or delete or report pornographic material involving a child and transmitting, displaying and distributing such material except for the purpose of reporting it is also punishable with fine.

In 2013, the Supreme Court in the case of *State of Kerala v. Shafin Jahan*, held that possession and circulation of child pornography are criminal offences under the POCSO Act. The court emphasized that the POCSO Act is a comprehensive legislation that seeks to protect children from sexual exploitation and abuse.

In 2018, the Supreme Court in the case of *Sabu Mathew George v. Union of India*, directed the government to take steps to block all websites that host child pornography. The court held that the right to freedom of speech and expression under the Constitution of India does not include the right to disseminate child pornography.

In 2019, the Supreme Court in the case of *Prajwala v. Union of India*, ordered the government to set up a dedicated nodal agency to tackle the problem of online child sexual abuse material. The court also directed the government to ensure that all law enforcement agencies are trained to handle cases of child sexual abuse.

To conclude, child pornography is a serious crime and a violation of the rights of the child. The POCSO Act provides a strong legal framework to deal with this issue, but more needs to be done to prevent and deter such crimes. It is the responsibility of everyone to work towards creating a safer environment for children and to ensure that their rights are protected.

Role of Parents, Teachers and Schools

CHAPTER **18**

What are the various parties that can play a role in sensitizing children about the POCSO Act?

Sensitizing children about the Protection of Children from Sexual Offences (POCSO) Act is an essential aspect of creating awareness and preventing child sexual abuse. Several parties can play a role in sensitizing children about the act, including:

- Parents: Parents can sensitize their children about the POCSO Act by discussing the issue at home and creating an open and safe space for their children to discuss any concerns they may have. Parents can also teach their children about good touch and bad touch and how to recognize and report any inappropriate behaviour.
- Schools: Schools play a critical role in educating children about the POCSO Act. Teachers can include age-appropriate information about the act in their curriculum, organize awareness workshops, and conduct special sessions on the topic.
- NGOs: Non-governmental organizations (NGOs) working in the field of child protection can organize awareness campaigns, workshops, and training sessions for children to sensitize them about the POCSO Act.
- Government agencies: Government agencies, such as the National Commission for Protection of Child Rights (NCPCR), can organize awareness programs and campaigns for children to educate them about the POCSO Act and their rights as a child.
- Media: The media can play a crucial role in sensitizing children about the POCSO Act by creating age-appropriate content and broadcasting it on television, radio, and social media platforms.

Creating awareness and sensitizing children about the POCSO Act is a collective effort, and various parties such as schools, parents, NGOs, government agencies, and the media can play a role in achieving this goal.

By working together, we can create a safe and protective environment for our children and prevent child sexual abuse.

Role of Parents:

Parents play a crucial role in the prevention of child sexual abuse and in ensuring that their children are protected from such heinous crimes. As per the Protection of Children from Sexual Offences Act (POCSO), parents have a legal obligation to safeguard their children from all forms of sexual abuse and exploitation. Here are some of the roles and responsibilities of parents under POCSO:

- Education: Parents should educate themselves and their children about body safety, safe and unsafe touch, and the importance of speaking up. They should also teach their children about boundaries and consent, so they can recognize when someone is crossing a line.
- Communication: Parents should maintain open and honest communication with their children, create a safe environment for them to share their feelings and experiences, and listen to their concerns without judgment. They should also encourage their children to ask questions and clarify doubts.
- Empowerment: Parents should empower their children by teaching them assertiveness skills, such as saying "no" and setting boundaries. They should also encourage their children to trust their instincts and to speak up if they feel uncomfortable or unsafe.
- Prevention: Parents can take preventive measures, such as not leaving their children alone with strangers or untrustworthy adults, teaching their children about internet safety and privacy, and ensuring that their children's schools and other activities have appropriate child protection policies.
- Creating Awareness: Parents need to educate their children about good touch and bad touch, and also about the dangers of sexual abuse. They should communicate with their children openly and encourage them to share any concerns or fears that they may have.
- Monitoring: Parents should monitor their child's behaviour and any changes in their demeanour, mood, unexplained injuries and secrecy or physical appearance. They should also observe any signs of discomfort or unease that their child may display in the company of certain individuals.

They should also be aware of the people their children interact with and the places they go to and monitor their online activities.

- Reporting: If parents suspect that their child has been a victim of sexual abuse or exploitation, they should immediately report the matter to the authorities. Delay in reporting such incidents can lead to further harm to the child and hinder the investigation.
- Support: If a child discloses abuse or experiences trauma, parents should provide emotional support and validation, help them access professional support and counselling, and report the abuse to the appropriate authorities. Parents should provide emotional support to their child and create a safe and supportive environment for them to express themselves. They should also seek professional help if required.

Role of Teachers and Schools:

Teachers and schools play a vital role in the prevention of child sexual abuse and in ensuring the safety and well-being of children. Here are some of the ways in which teachers and schools can help prevent child sexual abuse through POCSO:

- Conducting Body Safety Education: One of the most crucial roles of teachers and schools is to conduct Body Safety Education (POCSO) for children. This will enable children to understand what their private parts are, what constitutes safe and unsafe touch, and how to seek help if they experience any form of abuse. Teachers can use age-appropriate materials and techniques to make the learning experience engaging, interactive, and fun for children.
- Creating Safe and Inclusive Environments: Teachers and schools can create safe and inclusive environments by promoting a culture of respect, empathy, and inclusivity. This means creating an environment where children feel comfortable sharing their concerns or experiences without fear of judgment or retribution.
- Identifying Signs of Abuse: Teachers and school staff are often the first to notice signs of abuse in children. Therefore, it is essential to train teachers and staff to identify signs of abuse, such as changes in behaviour or mood, unexplained bruises or injuries, and inappropriate knowledge or behaviour regarding sex.

- Reporting Abuse: Teachers and school staff are mandated reporters, meaning that they have a legal obligation to report any instances or suspicions of child abuse. Teachers and staff should be trained to report abuse to the designated authorities and to follow the protocols and guidelines provided by their school or institution.
- Supporting Survivors: Teachers and schools can play a critical role in supporting survivors of abuse by providing them with a safe and supportive environment to share their experiences, offering emotional support and counselling services, and connecting them with appropriate resources and services.
- Advocating for Prevention: Teachers and schools can also play an important role in advocating for prevention of child sexual abuse by raising awareness, promoting policies and initiatives that prioritize child safety, and partnering with parents, caregivers, and community organizations to promote child safety.

The safety and protection of children from sexual abuse and exploitation are crucial, and both parents and teachers/schools play significant roles in achieving this. Parents can create awareness, monitor, report, and provide support to ensure their children's safety, while teachers and schools can promote child safety by conducting Body Safety Education, creating safe environments, identifying and reporting abuse, supporting survivors, and advocating for prevention. Ultimately, creating a safer society for children to grow and flourish requires a collective effort from all stakeholders.

CHAPTER

19

Increasing Awareness Through Games and Activities

Sample games and activities to educate children, parents, teachers, schools, and other agencies about POCSO and increase awareness are:

Games:

- "Good Touch, Bad Touch" Game: This is a simple game where children learn to identify appropriate and inappropriate touch. The game helps children understand what constitutes abuse and how to report it.
- "Safe Body, Safe Space" Game: This is a role-playing game that teaches children about personal boundaries and the concept of personal space. Children learn to respect others' personal space and understand that their own bodies are private.
- "Safe or Not Safe?" game: This is a simple guessing game where children are shown pictures of different situations and have to decide if they are safe or not. This can help children understand what constitutes a safe or unsafe situation.
- "Say No to Secrets" game: This is a conversation-based game where children learn about the importance of speaking up if someone asks them to keep a secret that makes them feel uncomfortable.
- "Who Can Help Me?" Game: This game teaches children about different sources of help, such as parents, teachers, and the police. It helps children understand that there are many people who can help them if they ever need it.
- "No, Go, Tell" Game: This game teaches children about the importance of saying "no" to inappropriate touch, "go" away from the situation, and "tell" a trusted adult about what happened. It emphasizes the importance of recognizing and understanding inappropriate behaviour and encourages children to speak up and seek help when needed.

- "Body Safety Bingo": This is a bingo game where children learn about body safety rules, such as no one should touch their private parts. This game designed to educate children about their bodies, appropriate and inappropriate touches, and the concept of body safety. This format aims to engage children in learning about different aspects of body safety, including identifying and understanding appropriate and inappropriate touches, setting boundaries, and recognizing signs of potential danger. The game encourages open discussions about personal boundaries, safe and unsafe touches, and how to respond in uncomfortable situations.
- "What Would You Do?" Game: A scenario-based game that helps children understand how to respond to situations that could lead to child sexual abuse. Parents, teachers, and schools can organize this game to teach children about the importance of speaking up and seeking help if they ever experience or witness abuse.

Activities:

- Role-playing: Children can act out different scenarios related to child sexual abuse and discuss what they would do in each situation. This activity helps children understand different perspectives and makes them think more deeply about the situation. Parents, teachers, and schools can all participate in this activity.
- Body Safety Education: Schools can organize workshops or classes to teach children about their bodies and how to keep them safe. This can include lessons on boundaries, consent, and what to do if someone makes them feel uncomfortable. Parents, teachers, and other agencies can also participate in these classes to learn how to educate children about body safety.
- Act and storytelling: Children can be encouraged to express their feelings about child sexual abuse through act or storytelling. This can be a great way for children to process their emotions and gain a deeper understanding of the issue. Schools, parents, and other agencies can participate in these activities to learn how to support children who have experienced abuse.
- Workshops with experts: Schools can invite experts in child protection and child psychology to give talks and conduct workshops on child sexual abuse. These workshops can provide children, parents, teachers, and other

agencies with a deeper understanding of the issue and give them the tools they need to stay safe.

- Storytelling sessions: Schools can organize storytelling sessions where children can listen to stories related to child sexual abuse and learn how to identify and report abuse. This can also help children understand the importance of seeking help if they ever need it. Parents, teachers, and other agencies can also participate in these sessions to learn how to support children who have experienced abuse.
- Awareness campaigns: Schools, parents, and other agencies can work together to organize awareness campaigns to educate the community about child sexual abuse and the importance of speaking up and seeking help. These campaigns can include posters, flyers, and other materials that provide information about POCSO and how to identify and report abuse.
- Community meetings: Schools, parents, and other agencies can organize community meetings to discuss the issue of child sexual abuse and to educate the community about POCSO. These meetings can provide a platform for community members to share their experiences and learn from each other.

It is important to note that while the game can be a valuable tool in educating children about child sexual abuse, it should only be used in a safe and supportive environment where children feel comfortable discussing sensitive topics. Children should also be encouraged to report any abuse they experience or witness, and to seek help if they ever need it.

CHAPTER

Games – Step by Step

20

"Good Touch, Bad Touch"

The "Good Touch, Bad Touch" game is a role-playing game that can help children learn about appropriate and inappropriate touching. Here is a step-by-step guide on how to play the game:

- ***Explain to the child***: Begin by explaining the concept of good and bad touch to the child in a way that they can understand. You can say, "A good touch is when someone touches you in a way that makes you feel happy and safe, like a hug from a parent or a high-five from a friend. A bad touch is when someone touches you in a way that makes you feel uncomfortable or scared." Also bad touch involves the touching of the private parts.
- ***Demonstrate different types of touches:*** Demonstrate different types of touches, such as a friendly pat on the back, a hug, a kiss on the cheek, and an inappropriate touch, such as touching private parts. Explain to the child that private parts are those that are covered by a bathing suit or underwear.
- ***Role-play***: Ask the child to act out different scenarios where they are touched in different ways and have them identify whether it was a good touch or a bad touch. For example, you could say, "Imagine you're playing with a friend, and they give you a high-five. Was that a good touch or a bad touch?" Then, you could give them a scenario where someone touches them inappropriately and ask them to identify it as a bad touch. By engaging in role-playing scenarios and discussions, children can learn about personal boundaries in a safe and supportive environment.
- ***Encourage discussion:*** Encourage the child to discuss their feelings and reactions to different types of touches. Ask them how they would feel if someone touched them in a certain way and what they would do if it made them feel uncomfortable.

- ***Reinforce the message***: Reinforce the message that it is important to tell a trusted adult if someone touches them inappropriately, and that they should never keep it a secret.

The "Good Touch, Bad Touch" game is a tool for teaching children about appropriate and inappropriate touching in a safe environment. It boosts their confidence and encourages them to voice their discomfort in unsettling situations. This game enhances their self-awareness and self-confidence, and teaches them to communicate their needs and boundaries effectively, a crucial skill for social interactions and relationships. Furthermore, it aids in preventing sexual abuse and exploitation by equipping children with the ability to identify and react to inappropriate behavior.

"Safe Body, Safe Space"

"Safe Body, Safe Space" is a game that parents can use to teach children about personal safety and protection from sexual abuse. Here are the steps to play the game:

- ***Step 1: Introduce the Game***

Explain the purpose of the game, which is to teach children about keeping their body safe and respecting personal space. Encourage children to participate by asking questions and sharing their own experiences.

- ***Step 2: Define Personal Space***

Start by defining personal space, which is the area around a person that they consider to be their own. Explain that everyone has the right to their personal space and that they should respect other people's personal space as well.

- ***Step 3: Demonstrate Body Safety***

Explain the concept of "safe body" and "unsafe body" parts. Demonstrate how to identify "safe body" parts by pointing to the body parts that are okay to touch or be touched by others. Also, explain how to identify "unsafe body" parts, which are private parts that should not be touched by anyone except the child themselves.

- ***Step 4: Play the Game***

The game involves the child standing in the middle of a circle made up of family members or friends. The child should then spin around and randomly point to someone in the circle, who will then take a step forward into the child's personal space. The child should then say "stop" when they feel that the person has entered their personal space. If the person has come too close, the child can ask them to take a step back. This reinforces the importance of respecting personal space.

➢ ***Step 5: Discuss the Game***

After the game, discuss with the child how they felt during the game and what they learned. Reinforce the importance of respecting personal space and "safe body" parts and encourage the child to speak up if someone makes them feel uncomfortable.

➢ ***Step 6: Recap and Follow-up***

Recap the main points of the game and encourage the child to practice what they learned in real-life situations. Also, remind them that they can always talk to a trusted adult if they have any questions or concerns.

Playing "Safe Body, Safe Space" can help children understand personal safety and protection from sexual abuse in a fun and interactive way. By teaching children to recognize and respect personal space, parents can help them build a foundation for healthy boundaries and relationships.

"Safe or Not Safe"

The "Safe or Not Safe?" game is a simple and effective way to educate children about the POCSO Act and personal safety using illustrations and different scenarios. Here's how to play the game:

- ***Prepare the materials.*** You will need a set of pictures or illustrations of different scenarios, such as a child playing at the park, a child walking home from school, a child talking to a stranger or a stranger offering chocolates to a child.
- ***Introduce the game to the child.*** Explain that the game is about deciding if different scenarios are safe or not safe, and that the goal is to learn about personal safety and the importance of being aware of potential dangers.
- ***Show each scenario.*** Show the child each scenario one at a time and ask them to decide if they think it is safe or not safe. If they are unsure, encourage them to use their intuition and their knowledge and understanding of the situation to make a decision.
- ***Discuss each scenario with the child.*** Talk about why they made the decision they did and explain why certain situations may be safe or not safe. Use this opportunity to reinforce important safety messages and answer any questions the child may have.

- ***Play all the scenarios.*** Continue playing the game until all the scenarios have been discussed.

This game is a fun and engaging way for children to learn about personal safety and the POCSO Act. By playing the game regularly, children will develop a stronger understanding of what constitutes a safe or unsafe situation, and they will be better equipped to make good decisions about their personal safety.

"Say No to Secrets"

It is a game or initiative related to educating children about preventing sexual offenses or promoting awareness about the importance of disclosing such incidents, it could be a positive development. Here is a step-by-step guide for playing the "Say No to Secrets" game with your child:

- Start by explaining to your child that it's important to talk about things that make them feel uncomfortable or worried. Tell them that sometimes people might ask them to keep secrets that make them feel bad, and that it's okay to say no to these requests.
- Ask your child if they understand what a secret is, and if they can give you an example of a secret that they might be asked to keep.
- Explain that there are good secrets, like surprise parties, and bad secrets, like secrets that make them feel uncomfortable or scared.
- Ask your child to give examples of good and bad secrets.
- Play a role-playing game where you ask your child to imagine that someone has asked them to keep a secret that makes them feel uncomfortable. Ask them to practice saying "no" to the request and encourage them to be firm and confident.
- Talk about different scenarios where someone might ask your child to keep a secret, such as if someone touches them inappropriately, or if someone gives them something they shouldn't have.
- Encourage your child to come to you or another trusted adult if someone asks them to keep a bad secret. Remind them that they won't be in trouble for telling the truth, and that it's important to speak up if they feel unsafe.
- Wrap up the game by asking your child how they feel about saying no to bad secrets, and if they have any questions or concerns.

Here are a few examples of scenarios that you can use in the "Say No to Secrets" game:

- Imagine that a family friend gives your child a gift and asks them not to tell their parents about it.
- Imagine that someone asks your child to keep a secret about something that happened to them that makes them feel uncomfortable or scared.
- Imagine that someone touches your child inappropriately and asks them to keep it a secret.
- Imagine that someone offers your child a treat or a toy and asks them not to tell anyone.
- Imagine that someone shows your child something on their phone or computer that makes them feel uncomfortable and asks them to keep it a secret.

Remember, the goal of this game is to help your child understand the importance of speaking up and saying no to secrets that make them feel uncomfortable. Be sure to create a safe and supportive environment for your child to talk about their feelings and concerns and encourage open communication at all times.

"Who Can Help Me"

"Who Can Help Me?" is a game that can be used to help children learn about the different people and organizations that can help them if they are ever in an unsafe situation. Here are the steps to play the game:

- ***Explain the game***

Tell your child that you're going to play a game that will help them learn about the different people and organizations that can help them if they ever feel unsafe or uncomfortable.

- ***Brainstorm the helpers***

Brainstorm a list of people and organizations that can help children in need, such as parents, teachers, police officers, doctors, counsellors, child helpline numbers, and NGOs working for child welfare. Write each helper on a separate card or piece of paper.

- ***Shuffle and draw***

Shuffle the cards and place them face down on the table. Ask your child to pick a card and read it aloud.

- ***Discuss the helper***

Discuss with your child what that helper does and how they can help. For example, if your child draws a police officer card, you can explain that police officers are there to protect people and enforce the law. You can also explain how to contact them in an emergency.

- ***Repeat and revise***

Repeat steps 3 and 4 until all the cards have been drawn. You can revise any helpers your child is not familiar with and answer any questions they may have.

- ***Practice scenarios***

To reinforce the lessons learned from the game, practice different scenarios with your child where they might need help. For example, you could act out a situation where your child is lost in a crowded place and needs to find a police officer for help.

Playing the "Who Can Help Me?" game can help children feel more confident and empowered when it comes to their personal safety. It's important to remind them that they can always speak up and ask for help if they ever feel uncomfortable or in danger.

"No, Go, Tell"

The "No, Go, Tell" game is designed to teach children about personal safety and how to respond if they are approached inappropriately. The game is specifically designed to educate children about the Prevention of Children from Sexual Offences (POCSO) Act in India. Here are the step-by-step instructions for playing the game:

- ***Step 1:*** Gather a group of children and introduce the concept of personal safety. Explain to them that there are certain things that are not okay for anyone to do to them, and that they should always tell a trusted adult if someone does something that makes them uncomfortable.
- ***Step 2:*** Explain to the children in simple terms, such as telling them that it is a law that protects children from sexual abuse and that it is important for them to know what to do if someone tries to touch them inappropriately.
- ***Step 3:*** Explain the three key phrases of the "No, Go, Tell" game to the children:

  "No" means that if someone tries to touch you inappropriately, you should say "no" and try to get away from them.

"Go" means that if someone tries to touch you inappropriately and you can't get away, you should try to run away and find a safe place.
"Tell" means that after you have said "no" and/or gotten away, you should tell a trusted adult what happened.

- ***Step 4:*** Play a game of "No, Go, Tell" with the children. In this game, one child pretends to be the "tricky person" who is trying to touch the other children inappropriately. The other children practice saying "no," running away (if possible), and telling a trusted adult what happened.
- ***Step 5:*** After the game, ask the children if they have any questions or if there is anything they want to discuss. Encourage them to talk about their feelings and reassure them that they can always come to you or another trusted adult if they ever feel unsafe or uncomfortable.
- ***Step 6:*** Remind the children that the "No, Go, Tell" game is not a substitute for the POCSO Act or for talking to a trusted adult if they ever feel uncomfortable or unsafe. Encourage them to speak up and seek help if they ever need it.

By playing the "No, Go, Tell" game and discussing the POCSO Act with children, we can help to educate them about personal safety and empower them to protect themselves from potential harm.

"Body Safety Bingo"

"Body Safety Bingo" is a bingo game designed to teach children about personal safety, including how to protect themselves from sexual abuse. Step-by-step instructions for playing "Body Safety Bingo" are as follows:

- ***Create a bingo card:*** Create a bingo card with different body safety rules or messages on each square. Examples of body safety rules include "No one should touch your private parts," "Say no if someone makes you uncomfortable," "Tell a trusted adult if someone touches you inappropriately," etc.
- ***Explain the rules:*** Explain to the children that the game is like regular bingo, but instead of numbers, the squares have body safety rules on them. Tell them that they can mark off a square when they learn about that rule.
- ***Discuss the rules:*** Discuss each body safety rule with the children and make sure they understand what it means. Answer any questions they may have and provide examples to help them understand.

- ***Play the game:*** Give each child a bingo card and some markers (such as stickers or pens). Call out the body safety rules one by one, and the children can mark off the corresponding square if they have it on their card. The first person to get a line of marked squares (horizontal, vertical, or diagonal) yells out "Bingo!" and wins the game.
- ***Reinforce the rules:*** After the game, reinforce the body safety rules and make sure the children understand the importance of following them. Remind them that if they ever feel uncomfortable or if someone touches them inappropriately, they should tell a trusted adult right away.

Playing "Body Safety Bingo" can be a fun and interactive way to teach children about personal safety and the importance of protecting themselves from sexual abuse.

"What Would You Do?"

This game is a scenario-based game designed to educate children on child sexual abuse and help them understand how to respond to such situations. The game presents children with various situations related to child sexual abuse and asks them to decide on what they would do in each situation.

Here's how the game is played:

- The teacher or facilitator presents a scenario related to child sexual abuse to the children.
- Children are asked to think about what they would do in the scenario and decide on the best course of action.
- Children can discuss their decisions with the facilitator or with the other children in the group. This helps children understand different perspectives and makes them think more deeply about the situation.
- The facilitator can then explain what the correct course of action is and why. Children can also be given information on how to report abuse and who they can talk to if they ever need help.

Examples of scenarios that can be used in the "What Would You Do?" Game:

- A family member asks you to keep a secret from your parents that makes you feel uncomfortable.
- An adult offers you candy or a toy in exchange for a hug or a kiss.
- A friend touches your private parts when you're playing together.

- A stranger tries to take you away from a public place.
- A teacher asks you to keep sitting next to them during recess even though you don't want to.

The game helps children understand the importance of being able to recognize situations that could potentially lead to abuse and how to respond to them. It also helps children understand the importance of seeking help if they ever need it.

CHAPTER

21 Miscellaneous Judgements

The Supreme Court of India has delivered several landmark judgments related to the Protection of Children from Sexual Offences (POCSO) Act, 2012 since its enactment. Some of the latest landmark judgments are discussed below:

Attorney General for India v. Satish and another (2021)

This is a case where the Supreme Court of India overturned a Bombay High Court decision that held that skin-to-skin contact is necessary for a sexual assault charge under the POCSO Act. The case involved a man who was accused of groping a 12-year-old girl's breast over her clothes. The Supreme Court held that any act of touching with sexual intent without consent would amount to sexual assault under the POCSO Act, regardless of whether there was skin-to-skin contact or not. The court also said that such acts would have a serious impact on the dignity and bodily integrity of children.

The court set aside the acquittal of the accused by the Bombay High Court and restored his conviction and sentence by the trial court. The court also expressed its displeasure over the insensitive remarks made by some judges while dealing with cases involving sexual offences against women and children.

Independent Thought v. Union of India (2017)

This judgment was a significant milestone in the fight against child marriage and child sexual abuse. The case dealt with the issue of whether sexual intercourse with a minor wife between the ages of 15 and 18 years would amount to rape under the Indian Penal Code (IPC). The Supreme Court held that sexual intercourse with a wife below the age of 18 years would amount to rape under the IPC and would also be an offence under the POCSO Act.

The judgment clarified that the exception to the offence of rape under the IPC, which allows sexual intercourse with a wife between the ages of 15 and 18 years, would not apply to cases of child marriage. The court held that child marriage was illegal and violated the rights of the child to education, health, and development.

State of Madhya Pradesh v. Kalyan Singh (2020)

In this case, the Supreme Court dealt with the issue of whether the absence of penetrative sexual assault would preclude the offence of aggravated penetrative sexual assault under the POCSO Act. The court held that any sexual act with a child that involves physical contact and is invasive in nature would fall under the definition of aggravated penetrative sexual assault.

The court emphasized that the POCSO Act was enacted to protect children from sexual abuse and exploitation and that the definition of sexual assault should be interpreted broadly to achieve this objective.

State of Haryana v. Bhajan Lal (2021)

This case dealt with the issue of whether the absence of a medical examination report in a case of sexual assault would be fatal to the prosecution's case under the POCSO Act. The Supreme Court held that the absence of a medical examination report would not be fatal to the prosecution's case if other evidence, such as the testimony of the victim and the investigating officer, could establish the offence.

The court held that the POCSO Act was a special legislation enacted to protect children from sexual abuse and exploitation and that a strict interpretation of procedural requirements could not be used to defeat the purpose of the Act.

The State of Karnataka v. Umesh (2021)

This case dealt with the issue of whether the act of touching a child's private parts would amount to sexual assault under the POCSO Act. The Supreme Court held that any physical contact with a child that is sexual in nature and violates the child's right to privacy would amount to sexual assault under the POCSO Act.

The court emphasized that the POCSO Act was enacted to protect children from sexual abuse and exploitation and that the definition of sexual assault should be interpreted broadly to achieve this objective.

Subhash Kashinath Mahajan v. The State of Maharashtra (2018)

This case dealt with the issue of whether the offence of possessing child pornography would fall under the definition of sexual harassment under the POCSO Act. The Supreme Court held that possession of child pornography would fall under the definition of sexual harassment under the POCSO Act.

The court held that the POCSO Act was enacted to protect children from sexual abuse and exploitation and that possession of child pornography could have a harmful effect on the child's psyche and development.

State of Tamil Nadu v. R. Mathialagan (2020)

This case dealt with the issue of whether the offence of sexual assault under the POCSO Act would attract the provisions of the Scheduled Castes and Scheduled Tribes (Prevention of Atrocities) Act, 1989. The Supreme Court held that sexual assault on a child belonging to a Scheduled Caste or Scheduled Tribe would attract the provisions of the Scheduled Castes and Scheduled Tribes (Prevention of Atrocities) Act, 1989.

The court emphasized that the POCSO Act and the Scheduled Castes and Scheduled Tribes (Prevention of Atrocities) Act, 1989 were both enacted to protect vulnerable sections of society and that the offences under the two Acts could not be viewed in isolation.

State of Madhya Pradesh v. Vishnu Khandelwal (2018)

This case dealt with the issue of whether the failure of the prosecution to produce the victim's statement under Section 164 of the Criminal Procedure Code (CrPC) would be fatal to the prosecution's case under the POCSO Act. The Supreme Court held that the failure to produce the victim's statement under Section 164 of the CrPC would not be fatal to the prosecution's case if other evidence, such as the testimony of the victim and the investigating officer, could establish the offence.

The court emphasized that the POCSO Act was a special legislation enacted to protect children from sexual abuse and exploitation and that a strict interpretation of procedural requirements could not be used to defeat the purpose of the Act.

State of Kerala v. Rasheed (2021)

This case dealt with the issue of whether a child's consent could be a defence in a case of sexual assault under the POCSO Act. The Supreme Court held that a child's consent could not be a defence in a case of sexual assault under the POCSO Act.

The court held that the POCSO Act was enacted to protect children from sexual abuse and exploitation and that a child's consent could not be considered valid as the child was not capable of giving informed consent due to their age and vulnerability.

Alakh Alok Srivastava Vs Union of India and Others reported in 2018 SCC Online SC 478

The case of Alakh Alok Srivastava Vs Union of India and Others is a landmark judgement by the Supreme Court of India with regard to the implementation of the Protection of Children from Sexual Offences (POCSO) Act, 2012. The petitioner in this case, Alakh Alok Srivastava, a lawyer and child rights activist, filed a Public Interest Litigation (PIL) in 2018, seeking various directions from the court for the effective implementation of the POCSO Act. The PIL highlighted several issues such as delay in investigation and trial, lack of infrastructure and facilities, inadequate compensation to victims, and inadequate awareness about the POCSO Act among the general public.

The Supreme Court, in its judgement delivered on 22nd July 2019, acknowledged the importance of protecting children from sexual abuse and emphasized the need for effective implementation of the POCSO Act. The court directed the central and state governments to take various measures for the effective implementation of the Act, such as:

- *Setting up of Special Courts:* The court directed the Central and State governments to establish Special Courts for the speedy trial of cases under the POCSO Act. The court also directed that these courts should be equipped with child-friendly infrastructure and facilities.
- *Adequate compensation to victims:* The court directed that adequate compensation should be provided to the victims of sexual abuse under the POCSO Act. The compensation should cover the cost of medical treatment, rehabilitation, and education.
- *Sensitization and awareness:* The court directed the central and state governments to conduct awareness programs and sensitization workshops

to educate children, parents, teachers, and the general public about the POCSO Act and its provisions.

- *Standard Operating Procedures (SOPs):* The court directed the central and state governments to develop Standard Operating Procedures (SOPs) for the investigation and trial of cases under the POCSO Act. The SOPs should ensure the protection of the rights of the child victim and provide for the confidentiality of their identity.
- *Monitoring and Review:* The court directed the central and state governments to set up a monitoring mechanism to review the implementation of the POCSO Act at regular intervals.

The judgement of the Supreme Court in the Alakh Alok Srivastava case is a significant step towards the protection of children from sexual abuse. The directions given by the court are aimed at ensuring the effective implementation of the POCSO Act and providing a safe and secure environment for children. The judgement highlights the need for a collective effort by the government, civil society, and the general public to prevent and combat sexual abuse against children.

"24. ...We are absolutely conscious that Section 35(2) of the Act says, "as far as possible". Be that as it may, regard being had to the spirit of the Act, we think it appropriate to issue the following directions:—

i The High Courts shall ensure that the cases registered under the POCSO Act are tried and disposed of by the Special Courts and the presiding officers of the said courts are sensitized in the matters of child protection and psychological response.

ii The Special Courts, as conceived, be established, if not already done, and be assigned the responsibility to deal with the cases under the POCSO Act.

iii The instructions should be issued to the Special Courts to fast track the cases by not granting unnecessary adjournments and following the procedure laid down in the POCSO Act and thus complete the trial in a time-bound manner or within a specific time frame under the Act.

iv The Chief Justices of the High Courts are requested to constitute a Committee of three Judges to regulate and monitor the progress of the trials under the POCSO Act. The High Courts where three Judges are not available the Chief Justices of the said courts shall constitute one Judge Committee.

v The Director General of Police or the officer of equivalent rank of the States shall constitute a Special Task Force which shall ensure that the investigation is properly conducted, and witnesses are produced on the dates fixed before the trial courts.

vi Adequate steps shall be taken by the High Courts to provide child friendly atmosphere in the Special Courts keeping in view the provisions of the POCSO Act so that the spirit of the Act is observed."

State v. Sujeet Kumar, Criminal Application 1190 of 2014 (Delhi)

In **State v. Sujeet Kumar**, the Delhi High Court was critical of the inappropriate questions posed by a Magistrate to assess the competence of a two-and-a-half year old child victim of a brutal rape before recording her statement under Section 164, Cr. P.C. It found the questions to the child about the school she went to and the class she studied in highly inappropriate as the child lived in a slum and did not attend any school. The Magistrate then asked her if she understood the term "truth" and the difference between truth and lie. The High Court observed: "How could a two and half year-old child explain the meaning of word "truth" and state difference between truth and lie. It is very difficult, even for adults, to respond to abstract questions asking them to explain the conceptual difference between truth and lie. What to talk of a two and half year-old child."

The Delhi High Court cited an article "Child Witness Competency: When Should the Issue be Raised" and highlighted the key points as follows–

- Asking, "What does it mean to tell the truth?" and "What does it mean to tell a lie?" are more developmentally appropriate for young children than asking, "What is the difference between the truth and a lie?
- Very young children often are unable to answer even these easier questions in a narrative form due to their underdeveloped language skills. Situationally relevant multiple-choice questions can be posed to assess the child's competency.
- Examples of such questions are:
    - If I told your mom that you just yelled at me, would that be the truth or a lie?
    - If you told your mom that I hit you, would that be the truth or a lie?

   - If you told your teacher that something bad happened to you, but it really didn't happen-you were making it up-would you be telling the truth or a lie?

- Competent children should be able to consistently provide correct answers to these multiple-choice questions.

In conclusion, these landmark judgments have strengthened the legal framework for the protection of children from sexual abuse and exploitation under the POCSO Act. They have provided guidance and clarity on various issues related to the interpretation and implementation of the Act and emphasized the need for a child-centric approach in dealing with cases of sexual abuse against children.

CHAPTER

22

Challenges in Implementing the POCSO Act

The Protection of Children from Sexual Offences (POCSO) Act, 2012 is an essential legal instrument that aims to protect children from sexual abuse and exploitation in India. However, despite its well-intentioned provisions, the implementation of the Act has faced several challenges.

One of the most significant challenges in implementing the POCSO Act is the low conviction rates. The conviction rate in POCSO cases is only around 30%, which is much lower than the conviction rate in other criminal cases. This can be attributed to several reasons, such as the lack of forensic evidence, the reluctance of witnesses to testify, and the ineffective prosecution of cases. The low conviction rates often discourage victims from reporting cases, as they may feel that the legal system does not provide adequate protection.

Another challenge in implementing the Act is the lack of awareness among stakeholders. Many people, including parents, teachers, and law enforcement officials, are not familiar with the provisions of the Act and do not know how to identify or report cases of sexual abuse. This can lead to cases of abuse going unnoticed and unreported, which can have serious consequences for the victims.

Additionally, there is a need for better victim support services. Victims of sexual abuse often face social stigma and psychological trauma, which can have long-lasting effects on their mental health and well-being. The legal system needs to provide adequate support to victims, including counseling, medical care, and rehabilitation services, to help them recover from the trauma of abuse.

Another challenge is the hesitation of parents to report cases of sexual abuse due to concerns about the identity and reputation of their child. Many parents may fear that reporting cases could lead to social stigma or harm their child's reputation. It is essential to create a supportive environment where victims and their families feel safe and supported in reporting cases of sexual abuse.

To strengthen the implementation of the POCSO Act, there is a need for a comprehensive approach that addresses these challenges. This could involve measures such as increasing awareness among stakeholders about the Act, improving victim support services, providing better training to law enforcement officials, and ensuring effective prosecution of cases. It is essential to create a safe and supportive environment where victims feel comfortable reporting cases of sexual abuse and have access to adequate support services.

Overall, the POCSO Act is a crucial legal instrument that aims to protect children from sexual abuse and exploitation. Addressing the challenges in its implementation is essential to ensure that the Act effectively protects the rights and welfare of children.

CHAPTER

Helplines

23

There are several helplines available in India for reporting cases of child sexual abuse under the Protection of Children from Sexual Offences (POCSO) Act, 2012. Here are a few of the most prominent ones:

- Childline India Foundation: **1098** (National helpline for children in distress):

Childline India Foundation is a 24-hour national helpline for children in distress. It is a project of the Indian Ministry of Women and Child Development and is run by non-governmental organizations (NGOs) across the country. The helpline provides immediate assistance to children in need, including those who are victims of child sexual abuse. Information on this helpline, as well as the POCSO eBox, is now being published on the inside of the front cover of all course books from class 6-12, according to the Women and Child Development (WCD) Ministry.

- National Commission for Protection of Child Rights: 011-23478200/ 23478201

The National Commission for Protection of Child Rights (NCPCR) is a statutory body established under the Commission for Protection of Child Rights Act, 2005. It works towards ensuring the protection, development, and well-being of children in India. The helpline provides assistance to children in distress, including those who are victims of child sexual abuse.

- Ministry of Women and Child Development: 1800-11-3090

The Ministry of Women and Child Development is responsible for the formulation and implementation of policies and programs for the development and protection of women and children in India. The ministry operates a toll-free helpline to provide support and assistance to children who are victims of sexual abuse.

- Rape, Abuse & Incest National Network (RAINN): 001-800-656-HOPE (International helpline)

  RAINN is the largest anti-sexual violence organization in the United States. It operates a 24-hour helpline for victims of sexual assault, including child sexual abuse. The helpline provides free, confidential support and information to survivors of sexual violence.

- Save the Children: 9910566000 / 9910567000
  Save the Children is a global organization that works towards improving the lives of children in need. In India, the organization operates a helpline to provide support and assistance to children who are victims of sexual abuse.
- Child Helpline International: +31-20-528-9090 (International helpline)
  Child Helpline International is a global network of helplines for children in distress. It operates in more than 140 countries and provides support, assistance, and protection to children who are victims of abuse, including child sexual abuse.
- Child Rights and You (CRY): 1800-209-3222

Child Rights and You is an Indian NGO that works towards ensuring the rights of children are protected and upheld. The organization operates a helpline to provide support and assistance to children who are victims of sexual abuse.

- Bachpan Bachao Andolan: 1800-11-0011

Bachpan Bachao Andolan is an Indian NGO that works towards the prevention of child trafficking and exploitation. The organization operates a helpline to provide support and assistance to children who are victims of sexual abuse.

- Prayas: 0124-2335108

Prayas is an Indian NGO that works towards the welfare and development of children in need. The organization operates a helpline to provide support and assistance to children who are victims of sexual abuse.

- Kailash Satyarthi Children's Foundation: 011-41496100

The Kailash Satyarthi Children's Foundation is an Indian NGO founded by Nobel Peace Prize laureate Kailash Satyarthi. The organization works towards the protection and empowerment of children in India. The foundation operates a helpline to provide support and assistance to children who are victims of sexual abuse.

- POCSO e-Box: The POCSO e-Box is an online platform for reporting cases of child sexual abuse, providing a secure and anonymous way to report incidents. 1800115455(Toll free),9868235077,1098(Childline). The platform can be accessed through the website: https://ncpcr.gov.in/pocso/

The helplines for POCSO provide support, advice, and assistance to victims of child sexual abuse and their families. Reporting child sexual abuse is the responsibility of all adults, and it's crucial to contact the appropriate authorities if abuse is suspected. These helplines can help prevent further abuse and protect the child by providing early reporting and intervention. Furthermore, these helplines can offer support and guidance to those affected by child sexual abuse, helping them access resources and assistance to recover and move forward.

CHAPTER

Latest Amendments

24

On 11th August 2023, three bills were introduced in the Lok Sabha that sought to repeal and replace the Indian Penal Code, 1860, Code of Criminal Procedure, 1973, and the Indian Evidence Act, 1872. The three bills are:

- The Bharatiya Nyaya Sanhita, 2023: This bill aims to replace the Indian Penal Code, 1860, with a new law that reflects the contemporary values and aspirations of the Indian society. It also seeks to repeal the colonial-era law on sedition and introduce new offences such as armed rebellion, subversive and separatist activities, mob lynching, and rape of minors.
- The Bharatiya Nagarik Suraksha Sanhita, 2023: This bill aims to replace the Code of Criminal Procedure, 1973, with a new law that simplifies and streamlines the criminal justice process. It also seeks to introduce new provisions such as e-FIRs, trials in absentia, community service, and digitisation of the entire procedure.
- The Bharatiya Sakshya Bill, 2023: This bill aims to replace the Indian Evidence Act, 1872, with a new law that updates and modernises the rules of evidence. It also seeks to introduce new provisions such as mandatory forensic examination, video recording of statements, and protection of witnesses.

BSB, BNSS, and BNS-II were passed by both the houses of Parliament on December 20 and 21, 2023. The President gave his assent to all the three bills on December 25, 2023, making them Acts.

The new set of laws is aimed at complete overhaul of the prevailing criminal justice system in the country. The newly enacted Bharatiya Nyaya Sanhita, 2023, Bharatiya Nagarik Suraksha Sanhita, 2023 and Bharatiya Sakshya Adhiniyam, 2023 which seek to replace the Indian Penal Code(IPC), the Criminal Procedure Code (CrPC), 1973 and the Indian Evidence Act, 1972 respectively will come into force across the country from 1 July, 2024.

RELEVANT KEY CLAUSES:

The Bharatiya Nyaya Sanhita, 2023:

63. A man is said to commit "rape" if he—

(a) penetrates his penis, to any extent, into the vagina, mouth, urethra or anus ofa woman or makes her to do so with him or any other person; or

(b) inserts, to any extent, any object or a part of the body, not being the penis, into the vagina, the urethra or anus of a woman or makes her to do so with him or any other person; or

(c) manipulates any part of the body of a woman so as to cause penetration into the vagina, urethra, anus or any part of body of such woman or makes her to do so with him or any other person; or

(d) applies his mouth to the vagina, anus, urethra of a woman or makes her to doso with him or any other person, under the circumstances falling under any of the following seven descriptions:—

(i) against her will;

(ii) without her consent;

(iii) with her consent, when her consent has been obtained by putting her or any person in whom she is interested, in fear of death or of hurt;

(iv) with her consent, when the man knows that he is not her husband and that her consent is given because she believes that he is another man to whom she is or believes herself to be lawfully married;

(v) with her consent when, at the time of giving such consent, by reason of unsoundness of mind or intoxication or the administration by him personally or through another of any stupefying or unwholesome substance, she is unable to understand the nature and consequences of that to which she gives consent;

(vi) with or without her consent, when she is under eighteen years of age;

(vii) when she is unable to communicate consent.

Explanation 1.—For the purposes of this section, "vagina" shall also include labia majora. Explanation 2.—Consent means an unequivocal voluntary agreement when the woman by words, gestures or any form of verbal or non-verbal communication, communicates willingness to participate in the specific sexual act:

Provided that a woman who does not physically resist to the act of penetration shall not by the reason only of that fact, be regarded as consenting to the sexual activity.

Exception 1.—A medical procedure or intervention shall not constitute rape.

Exception 2.—Sexual intercourse or sexual acts by a man with his own wife, the wife not being under eighteen years of age, is not rape.

70. (1) Where a woman is raped by one or more persons constituting a group or acting in furtherance of a common intention, each of those persons shall be deemed to have committed the offence of rape and shall be punished with rigorous imprisonment for a term which shall not be less than twenty years, but which may extend to imprisonment for life which shall mean imprisonment for the remainder of that person's natural life, and with fine:

Provided that such fine shall be just and reasonable to meet the medical expenses and rehabilitation of the victim:

Provided further that any fine imposed under this sub-section shall be paid to the victim.

(2) Where a woman under eighteen years of age is raped by one or more persons constituting a group or acting in furtherance of a common intention, each of those persons shall be deemed to have committed the offence of rape and shall be punished with imprisonment for life, which shall mean imprisonment for the remainder of that person's natural life, and with fine, or with death:

Provided that such fine shall be just and reasonable to meet the medical expenses and rehabilitation of the victim:

Provided further that any fine imposed under this sub-section shall be paid to the victim.

93. Whoever hires, employs or engages any person below the age of eighteen years to commit an offence shall be punished with imprisonment of either description or fine provided for that offence as if the offence has been committed by such person himself.

Explanation.—Hiring, employing, engaging or using a child for sexual exploitation or pornography is covered within the meaning of this section.

96. Whoever sells, lets to hire, or otherwise disposes of child below eighteen years of age with intent that such child shall at any age be employed or used for the purpose of prostitution or illicit intercourse with any person or for any unlawful and immoral purpose, or knowing it to be likely that such person will at any age be employed or used for any such purpose, shall be punished with imprisonment of either description for a term which may extend to ten years, and shall also be liable to fine.

Explanation 1.—When a female under the age of eighteen years is sold, let for hire, or otherwise disposed of to a prostitute or to any person who keeps or manages a brothel, the person so disposing of such female shall, until the contrary is proved, be presumed to have disposed of her with the intent that she shall be used for the purpose of prostitution.

Explanation 2.—For the purposes of this section "illicit intercourse" means sexual intercourse between persons not united by marriage or by any union or tie which, though not amounting to a marriage, is recognised by the personal law or custom of the community to which they belong or, where they belong to different communities, of both such communities, as constituting between them a quasi-marital relation.

97. Whoever buys, hires or otherwise obtains possession of any child below the age of eighteen years with intent that such person shall at any age be employed or used for the purpose of prostitution or illicit intercourse with any person or for any unlawful and immoral purpose, or knowing it to be likely that such child will at any age be employed or used for any such purpose, shall be punished with imprisonment of either description for a term which shall not be less than seven years but which may extend to fourteen years, and shall also be liable to fine.

Explanation 1.—Any prostitute or any person keeping or managing a brothel, who buys, hires or otherwise obtains possession of a female under the age of eighteen years shall, until the contrary is proved, be presumed to have obtained possession of such female with the intent that she shall be used for the purpose of prostitution.

Explanation 2.—“Illicit intercourse” has the same meaning as in section 96.

The Bharatiya Nagarik Suraksha Sanhita, 2023:

193. (1) Every investigation under this Chapter shall be completed without unnecessary delay.

(2) The investigation in relation to an offence under sections 64, 66, 67, 68, 70, 71 of the Bharatiya Nyaya Sanhita, 2023 or under sections 4, 6, 8 or section 10 of the Protection of Children from Sexual Offences Act, 2012 shall be completed within two months from the date on which the information was recorded by the officer in charge of the police station.

366. (1) The place in which any Criminal Court is held for the purpose of inquiring into or trying any offence shall be deemed to be an open Court, to which the public generally may have access, so far as the same can conveniently contain them:

Provided that the presiding Judge or Magistrate may, if he thinks fit, order at any stage of any inquiry into, or trial of, any particular case, that the public generally, or any particular person, shall not have access to, or be or remain in, the room or building used by the Court.

(2) Notwithstanding anything contained in sub-section (1), the inquiry into and trial of rape or an offence under section 64, section 66, section 67, section 68, section 70 or section 71 of the Bharatiya Nyaya Sanhita, 2023 or under sections 4, 6, 8 or section 10 of the Protection of Children from Sexual Offences Act, 2012 shall be conducted in camera:

Provided that the presiding Judge may, if he thinks fit, or on an application made by either of the parties, allow any particular person to have access to, or be or remain in, the room or building used by the Court: Provided further that in camera trial shall be conducted as far as practicable by a woman Judge or Magistrate.

(3) Where any proceedings are held under sub-section (2), it shall not be lawful for any person to print or publish any matter in relation to any such proceedings except with the previous permission of the Court: Provided that the ban on printing or publication of trial proceedings

in relation to an offence of rape may be lifted, subject to maintaining confidentiality of name and address of the parties.

397. All hospitals, public or private, whether run by the Central Government, the State Government, local bodies or any other person, shall immediately, provide the first-aid or medical treatment, free of cost, to the victims of any offence covered under section 122, section 64, section 66, section 67, section 68, section 70, section 71 or section 122 of the Bharatiya Nyaya, Sanhita, 2023 or under sections 4, 6, 8 or section 10 of the Protection of Children from Sexual Offences Act, 2012, and shall immediately inform the police of such incident.

398. Every State Government shall prepare and notify a Witness Protection Scheme for the State with a view to ensure protection of the witnesses.

CHAPTER

25

Protection of Children from Sexual Offences Act, 2012

PREAMBLE - THE PROTECTION OF CHILDREN FROM SEXUAL OFFENCES ACT, 2012

PREAMBLE

An Act to protect children from offences of sexual assault, sexual harassment and pornography and provide for establishment of Special Courts for trial of such offences and for matters connected therewith or incidental thereto.

Whereas clause (3) of article 15 of the Constitution, inter alia, empowers the State to make special provisions for children;

And whereas, the Government of India has acceded on the 11th December, 1992 to the Convention on the Rights of the Child, adopted by the General Assembly of the United Nations, which has prescribed a set of standards to be followed by all State parties in securing the best interests of the child;

And whereas it is necessary for the proper development of the child that his or her right to privacy and confidentiality be protected and respected by every person by all means and through all stages of a judicial process involving the child;

And whereas it is imperative that the law operates in a manner that the best interest and well being of the child are regarded as being of paramount importance at every stage, to ensure the healthy physical, emotional, intellectual and social development of the child;

And whereas the State parties to the Convention on the Rights of the Child are required to undertake alt appropriate national, bilateral and multilateral measures to prevent—

(a) the inducement or coercion of a child to engage in any unlawful sexual activity;
(b) the exploitative use of children in prostitution or other unlawful sexual practices;
(c) the exploitative use of children in pornographic performances and materials; And whereas sexual exploitation and sexual abuse of children are heinous crimes and need to be effectively addressed.

Be it enacted by Parliament in the Sixty-third Year of the Republic of India as follows:-

Section 1 - Short title, extent and commencement

(1) This Act may be called the Protection of Children from Sexual Offences Act, 2012.
(2) It extends to the whole of India, [2][***].
(3) It shall come into force on such date as the Central Government may, by notification in the Official Gazette, appoint.

Section 2 - Definitions

(1) In this Act, unless the context otherwise requires, —
   (a) "aggravated penetrative sexual assault" has the same meaning as assigned to it in section 5;
   (b) "aggravated sexual assault" has the same meaning as assigned to it in section 9;
   (c) "armed forces or security forces" means armed forces of the Union or security forces or police forces, as specified in the Schedule;
   (d) "child" means any person below the age of eighteen years;
   [3][(da) "child pornography" means any visual depiction of sexually explicit conduct involving a child which include photograph, video, digital or computer generated image indistinguishable from an actual child and image created, adapted, or modified, but appear to depict a child;]

---

2. Omitted by Jammu And Kashmir Reorganisation Act, 2019, w.e.f. 31.10.2019 the previous text was:- "except the State of Jammu and Kashmir"

3. Inserted by Protection Of Children From Sexual Offences (Amendment) Act, 2019, w.e.f. 16.08.2019.

(e) "domestic relationship" shall have the same meaning as assigned to it in clause (f) of section 2 of the Protection of Women from Domestic Violence Act, 2005(43 of 2005);

(f) "penetrative sexual assault" has the same meaning as assigned to it in section 3;

(g) "prescribed" means prescribed by rules made under this Act;

(h) "religious institution" shall have the same meaning as assigned to it in the Religious Institutions (Prevention of Misuse) Act, 1988(41 of 1988);

(i) "sexual assault" has the same meaning as assigned to it in section 7;

(j) "sexual harassment" has the same meaning as assigned to it in section 11;

(k) "shared household" means a household where the person charged with the offence lives or has lived at any time in a domestic relationship with the child;

(l) "Special Court" means a court designated as such under section 28;

(m) "Special Public Prosecutor" means a Public Prosecutor appointed under section 32.

(2) The words and expressions used herein and not defined but defined in the Indian Penal Code(45 of 1860), the Code of Criminal Procedure, 1973(2 of 1974),[4] [the Juvenile Justice (Care and Protection of Children) Act, 2015 (2 of 2016)] and the Information Technology Act, 2000 (21 of 2000) shall have the meanings respectively assigned to them in the said Codes or the Acts.

Section 3 - Penetrative sexual assault

A person is said to commit "penetrative sexual assault" if—

(a) he penetrates his penis, to any extent, into the vagina, mouth, urethra or anus of a child or makes the child to do so with him or any other person; or

(b) he inserts, to any extent, any object or a part of the body, not being the penis, into the vagina, the urethra or anus of the child or makes the child to do so with him or any other person; or

---

4. Substituted by Protection Of Children From Sexual Offences (Amendment) Act, 2019, w.e.f. 16.08.2019 for the following:- "the Juvenile Justice (Care and Protection of Children) Act, 2000 (56 of 2000)"

(c) he manipulates any part of the body of the child so as to cause penetration into the vagina, urethra, anus or any part of body of the child or makes the child to do so with him or any other person; or

(d) he applies his mouth to the penis, vagina, anus, urethra of the child or makes the child to do so to such person or any other person.

Section 4 - Punishment for penetrative sexual assault

[15][(1)] Whoever commits penetrative sexual assault shall be punished with imprisonment of either description for a term which shall not be less than [6][ten years] but which may extend to imprisonment for life, and shall also be liable to fine.

[7][(2) Whoever commits penetrative sexual assault on a child below sixteen years of age shall be punished with imprisonment for a term which shall not be less than twenty years, but which may extend to imprisonment for life, which shall mean imprisonment for the remainder of natural life of that person and shall also be liable to fine.

(3) The fine imposed under sub-section (1) shall be just and reasonable and paid to the victim to meet the medical expenses and rehabilitation of such victim.]

1. Renumbered by Protection Of Children From Sexual Offences (Amendment) Act, 2019, w.e.f. 16.08.2019 for the following:- "(1)"
2. Substituted by Protection Of Children From Sexual Offences (Amendment) Act, 2019, w.e.f. 16.08.2019 for the following:- "seven years"
3. Inserted by Protection Of Children From Sexual Offences (Amendment) Act, 2019, w.e.f. 16.08.2019.

Section 5 - Aggravated penetrative sexual assault

(a) Whoever, being a police officer, commits penetrative sexual assault on a child—

(i) within the limits of the police station or premises at which he is appointed; or

---

5.

6.

7.

(ii) in the premises of any station house, whether or not situated in the police station, to which he is appointed; or

(iii) in the course of his duties or otherwise; or

(iv) where he is known as, or identified as, a police officer; or

(b) whoever being a member of the armed forces or security forces commits penetrative sexual assault on a child—

(i) within the limits of the area to which the person is deployed; or

(ii) in any areas under the command of the forces or armed forces; or

(iii) in the course of his duties or otherwise; or

(iv) where the said person is known or identified as a member of the security or armed forces; or

(c) whoever being a public servant commits penetrative sexual assault on a child; or

(d) whoever being on the management or on the staff of a jail, remand home, protection home, observation home, or other place of custody or care and protection established by or under any law for the time being in force, commits penetrative sexual assault on a child, being inmate of such jail, remand home, protection home, observation home, or other place of custody or care and protection; or

(e) whoever being on the management or staff of a hospital, whether Government or private, commits penetrative sexual assault on a child in that hospital; or

(f) whoever being on the management or staff of an educational institution or religious institution, commits penetrative sexual assault on a child in that institution; or

(g) whoever commits gang penetrative sexual assault on a child.

Explanation.—When a child is subjected to sexual assault by one or more persons of a group in furtherance of their common intention, each of such persons shall be deemed to have committed gang penetrative sexual assault within the meaning of this clause and each of such person shall be liable for that act in the same manner as if it were done by him alone; or

(h) whoever commits penetrative sexual assault on a child using deadly weapons, fire, heated substance or corrosive substance; or

(i) whoever commits penetrative sexual assault causing grievous hurt or causing bodily harm and injury or injury to the sexual organs of the child; or

(j) whoever commits penetrative sexual assault on a child, which—

(i) physically incapacitates the child or causes the child to become mentally ill as defined under clause (b) of section 2 of the Mental Health Act, 1987(14 of 1987) or causes impairment of any kind so as to render the child unable to perform regular tasks, temporarily or permanently; [81][***]

(ii) in the case of female child, makes the child pregnant as a consequence of sexual assault;

(iii) inflicts the child with Human Immunodeficiency Virus or any other life threatening disease or infection which may either temporarily or permanently impair the child by rendering him physically incapacitated, or mentally ill to perform regular tasks; [91][***]

[102][(iv) causes death of the child; or]

(k) whoever, taking advantage of a child's mental or physical disability, commits penetrative sexual assault on the child; or

(l) whoever commits penetrative sexual assault on the child more than once or repeatedly; or

(m) whoever commits penetrative sexual assault on a child below twelve years; or

(n) whoever being a relative of the child through blood or adoption or marriage or guardianship or in foster care or having a domestic relationship with a parent of the child or who is living in the same or shared household with the child, commits penetrative sexual assault on such child; or

(o) whoever being, in the ownership, or management, or staff, of any institution providing services to the child, commits penetrative sexual assault on the child; or

(p) whoever being in a position of trust or authority of a child commits penetrative sexual assault on the child in an institution or home of the child or anywhere else; or

(q) whoever commits penetrative sexual assault on a child knowing the child is pregnant; or

(r) whoever commits penetrative sexual assault on a child and attempts to murder the child; or

---

8.

9.

10.

(s) whoever commits penetrative sexual assault on a child in the course of [11]3[communal or sectarian violence or during any natural calamity or in similar situations]; or

(t) whoever commits penetrative sexual assault on a child and who has been previously convicted of having committed any offence under this Act or any sexual offence punishable under any other law for the time being in force; or

(u) whoever commits penetrative sexual assault on a child and makes the child to strip or parade naked in public, is said to commit aggravated penetrative sexual assault.

1. Omitted by Protection Of Children From Sexual Offences (Amendment) Act, 2019, w.e.f. 16.08.2019 the previous text was:- "or"
2. Inserted by Protection Of Children From Sexual Offences (Amendment) Act, 2019, w.e.f. 16.08.2019.
3. Substituted by Protection Of Children From Sexual Offences (Amendment) Act, 2019, w.e.f. 16.08.2019 for the following:- "communal or sectarian violence"

Section 6 - Punishment for aggravated penetrative sexual assault

[12]1 **[6. Punishment for aggravated penetrative sexual assault**

(1) Whoever commits aggravated penetrative sexual assault shall be punished with rigorous imprisonment for a term which shall not be less than twenty years, but which may extend to imprisonment for life, which shall mean imprisonment for the remainder of natural life of that person and shall also be liable to fine, or with death.

(2) The fine imposed under sub-section (1) shall be just and reasonable and paid to the victim to meet the medical expenses and rehabilitation of such victim.]

1. Substituted by Protection Of Children From Sexual Offences (Amendment) Act, 2019, w.e.f. 16.08.2019 for the following:-

"Whoever, commits aggravated penetrative sexual assault, shall be punished with rigorous imprisonment for a term which shall not be less than ten years but which may extend to imprisonment for life and shall also be liable to fine."

11.

12.

Section 7 - Sexual assault

Whoever, with sexual intent touches the vagina, penis, anus or breast of the child or makes the child touch the vagina, penis, anus or breast of such person or any other person, or does any other act with sexual intent which involves physical contact without penetration is said to commit sexual assault.

Section 8 - Punishment for sexual assault

Whoever, commits sexual assault, shall be punished with imprisonment of either description for a term which shall not be less than three years but which may extend to five years, and shall also be liable to fine.

Section 9 - Aggravated sexual assault

(a) Whoever, being a police officer, commits sexual assault on a child—
(i) within the limits of the police station or premises where he is appointed; or
(ii) in the premises of any station house whether or not situated in the police station to which he is appointed; or
(iii) in the course of his duties or otherwise; or
(iv) where he is known as, or identified as a police officer; or
(b) whoever, being a member of the armed forces or security forces, commits sexual assault on a child—
(i) within the limits of the area to which the person is deployed; or
(ii) in any areas under the command of the security or armed forces; or
(iii) in the course of his duties or otherwise; or
(iv) where he is known or identified as a member of the security or armed forces; or
(c) whoever being a public servant commits sexual assault on a child; or
(d) whoever being on the management or on the staff of a jail, or remand home or protection home or observation home, or other place of custody or care and

protection established by or under any law for the time being in force commits sexual assault on a child being inmate of such jail or remand home or protection home or observation home or other place of custody or care and protection; or
(e) whoever being on the management or staff of a hospital, whether Government or private, commits sexual assault on a child in that hospital; or

(f) whoever being on the management or staff of an educational institution or religious institution, commits sexual assault on a child in that institution; or

(g) whoever commits gang sexual assault on a child.

Explanation.—when a child is subjected to sexual assault by one or more persons of a group in furtherance of their common intention, each of such persons shall be deemed to have committed gang sexual assault within the meaning of this clause and each of such person shall be liable for that act in the same manner as if it were done by him alone; or

(h) whoever commits sexual assault on a child using deadly weapons, fire, heated substance or corrosive substance; or

(i) whoever commits sexual assault causing grievous hurt or causing bodily harm and injury or injury to the sexual organs of the child; or

(j) whoever commits sexual assault on a child, which—

(i) physically incapacitates the child or causes the child to become mentally ill as defined under clause (l) of section 2 of the Mental Health Act, 1987(14 of 1987) or causes impairment of any kind so as to render the child unable to perform regular tasks, temporarily or permanently; or

(ii) inflicts the child with Human Immunodeficiency Virus or any other life threatening disease or infection which may either temporarily or permanently impair the child by rendering him physically incapacitated, or mentally ill to perform regular tasks; or

(k) whoever, taking advantage of a child's mental or physical disability, commits sexual assault on the child; or

(l) whoever commits sexual assault on the child more than once or repeatedly; or

(m) whoever commits sexual assault on a child below twelve years; or

(n) whoever, being a relative of the child through blood or adoption or marriage or guardianship or in foster care, or having domestic relationship with a parent of the child, or who is living in the same or shared household with the child, commits sexual assault on such child; or

(o) whoever, being in the ownership or management or staff, of any institution providing services to the child, commits sexual assault on the child in such institution; or

(p) whoever, being in a position of trust or authority of a child, commits sexual assault on the child in an institution or home of the child or anywhere else; or

(q) whoever commits sexual assault on a child knowing the child is pregnant; or
(r) whoever commits sexual assault on a child and attempts to murder the child; or
(s) whoever commits sexual assault on a child in the course of [131][communal or sectarian violence or during any natural calamity or in any similar situations]; or
(t) whoever commits sexual assault on a child and who has been previously convicted of having committed any offence under this Act or any sexual offence punishable under any other law for the time being in force; or
(u) whoever commits sexual assault on a child and makes the child to strip or parade naked in public, is said to commit aggravated sexual assault.
[142][(v) whoever persuades, induces, entices or coerces a child to get administered or administers or direct anyone to administer, help in getting administered any drug or hormone or any chemical substance, to a child with the intent that such child attains early sexual maturity;]

1. Substituted by Protection Of Children From Sexual Offences (Amendment) Act, 2019, w.e.f. 16.08.2019 for the following:- "communal or sectarian violence"
2. Inserted by Protection Of Children From Sexual Offences (Amendment) Act, 2019, w.e.f. 16.08.2019.

Section 10 - Punishment for aggravated sexual assault

9+++Whoever, commits aggravated sexual assault shall be punished with imprisonment of either description for a term which shall not be less than five years but which may extend to seven years, and shall also be liable to fine.

Section 11 - Sexual harassment

A person is said to commit sexual harassment upon a child when such person with sexual intent,—

(i) utters any word or makes any sound, or makes any gesture or exhibits any object or part of body with the intention that such word or sound shall be heard, or such gesture or object or part of body shall be seen by the child; or

13.

14.

(ii) makes a child exhibit his body or any part of his body so as it is seen by such person or any other person; or

(iii) shows any object to a child in any form or media for pornographic purposes; or

(iv) repeatedly or constantly follows or watches or contacts a child either directly or through electronic, digital or any other means; or

(v) threatens to use, in any form of media, a real or fabricated depiction through electronic, film or digital or any other mode, of any part of the body of the child or the involvement of the child in a sexual act; or

(vi) entices a child for pornographic purposes or gives gratification therefore.

Explanation,—Any question which involves "sexual intent" shall be a question of fact.

Section 12 - Punishment for sexual harassment

Whoever, commits sexual harassment upon a child shall be punished with imprisonment of either description for a term which may extend to three years and shall also be liable to fine.

Section 13 - Use of child for pornographic purposes

Whoever, uses a child in any form of media (including programme or advertisement telecast by television channels or internet or any other electronic form or printed form, whether or not such programme or advertisement is intended for personal use or for distribution), for the purposes of sexual gratification, which includes—

(a) representation of the sexual organs of a child;

(b) usage of a child engaged in real or simulated sexual acts (with or without penetration);

(c) the indecent or obscene representation of a child,

shall be guilty of the offence of using a child for pornographic purposes.

Explanation.—For the purposes of this section, the expression "use a child" shall include involving a child through any medium like print, electronic, computer or any other technology for preparation, production, offering, transmitting, publishing, facilitation and distribution of the pornographic material.

Section 14 - Punishment for using child for pornographic purposes

14. Punishment for using child for pornographic purposes

[15][1][(1) Whoever uses a child or children for pornographic purposes shall be punished with imprisonment for a term which shall not be less than five years and shall also be liable to fine and in the event of second or subsequent conviction with imprisonment for a term which shall not be less than seven years and also be liable to fine.

(2) Whoever using a child or children for pornographic purposes under sub-section (1), commits an offence referred to in section 3 or section 5 or section 7 or section 9 by directly participating in such pornographic acts, shall be punished for the said offences also under section 4, section 6, section 8 and section 10, respectively, in addition to the punishment provided in sub-section (1).]

1. Substituted by Protection Of Children From Sexual Offences (Amendment) Act, 2019, w.e.f. 16.08.2019 for the following:-

"(1) Whoever, uses a child or children for pornographic purposes shall be punished with imprisonment of either description which may extend to five years and shall also be liable to fine and in the event of second or subsequent conviction with imprisonment of either description for a term which may extend to seven years and also be liable to fine.

(2) If the person using the child for pornographic purposes commits an offence referred to in section 3, by directly participating in pornographic acts, he shall be punished with imprisonment of either description for a term which shall not be less than ten years but which may extend to imprisonment for life, and shall also be liable to fine.

(3) If the person using the child for pornographic purposes commits an offence referred to in section 5, by directly participating in pornographic acts, he shall be punished with rigorous imprisonment for life and shall also be liable to fine.

(4) If the person using the child for pornographic purposes commits an offence referred to in section 7, by directly participating in pornographic acts, he shall be punished with imprisonment of either description for a

15.

term which shall not be less than six years but which may extend to eight years, and shall also be liable to fine.

(5) If the person using the child for pornographic purposes commits an offence referred to in section 9, by directly participating in pornographic acts, he shall be punished with imprisonment of either description for a term which shall not be less than eight years but which may extend to ten years, and shall also be liable to fine."

Section 15 - Punishment for storage of pornographic material involving child

[16]1[15. Punishment for storage of pornographic material involving child

(1) Any person, who stores or possesses pornographic material in any form involving a child, but fails to delete or destroy or report the same to the designated authority, as may be prescribed, with an intention to share or transmit child pornography, shall be liable to fine not less than five thousand rupees and in the event of second or subsequent offence, with fine which shall not be less than ten thousand rupees.

(2) Any person, who stores or possesses pornographic material in any form involving a child for transmitting or propagating or displaying or distributing in any manner at any time except for the purpose of reporting, as may be prescribed, or for use as evidence in court, shall be punished with imprisonment of either description which may extend to three years, or with fine, or with both.

(3) Any person, who stores or possesses pornographic material in any form involving a child for commercial purpose shall be punished on the first conviction with imprisonment of either description which shall not be less than three years which may extend to five years, or with fine, or with both and in the event of second or subsequent conviction, with imprisonment of either description which shall not be less than five years which may extend to seven years and shall also be liable to fine.]

16.

1. Substituted by Protection Of Children From Sexual Offences (Amendment) Act, 2019, w.e.f. 16.08.2019 for the following:-

"Any person, who stores, for commercial purposes any pornographic material in any form involving a child shall be punished with imprisonment of either description which may extend to three years or with fine or with both."

Section 16 - Abetment of an offence

A person abets an offence, who—

First.—Instigates any person to do that offence; or

Secondly.—Engages with one or more other person or persons in any conspiracy for the doing of that offence, if an act or illegal omission takes place in pursuance of that conspiracy, and in order to the doing of that offence; or

Thirdly.—Intentionally aids, by any act or illegal omission, the doing of that offence.

Explanation I.—A person who, by willful misrepresentation, or by willful concealment of a material fact, which he is bound to disclose, voluntarily causes or procures, or attempts to cause or procure a thing to be done, is said to instigate the doing of that offence.

Explanation II.—Whoever, either prior to or at the time of commission of an act, does anything in order to facilitate the commission of that act, and thereby facilitates the commission thereof, is said to aid the doing of that act.

Explanation III.—Whoever employ, harbours, receives or transports a child, by means of threat or use of force or other forms of coercion, abduction, fraud, deception, abuse of power or of a position, vulnerability or the giving or receiving of payments or benefits to achieve the consent of a person having control over another person, for the purpose of any offence under this Act, is said to aid the doing of that act.

Section 17 - Punishment for abetment

Whoever abets any offence under this Act, if the act abetted is committed in consequence of the abetment, shall be punished with punishment provided for that offence.

Explanation. — An act or offence is said to be committed in consequence of abetment, when it is committed in consequence of the instigation, or in pursuance of the conspiracy or with the aid, which constitutes the abetment.

Section 18 - Punishment for attempt to commit an offence

Whoever attempts to commit any offence punishable under this Act or to cause such an offence to be committed, and in such attempt, does any act towards the commission of the

offence, shall be punished with imprisonment of any description provided for the offence, for a term which may extend to one-half of the imprisonment for life or, as the case may be, one-half of the longest term of imprisonment provided for that offence or with fine or with both.

Section 19 - Reporting of offences

(1) Not withstanding anything contained in the Code of Criminal Procedure, 1973(2 of 1974), any person (including the child), who has apprehension that in offence under this Act is likely to be committed or has knowledge that such an offence has been committed, he shall provide such information to,—

(a) the Special Juvenile Police Unit; or

(b) the local police.

(2) Every report given under sub-section (1) shall be—

(a) ascribed an entry number and recorded in writing;

(b) be read over to the informant;

(c) shall be entered in a book to be kept by the Police Unit

(3) Where the report under sub-section (1) is given by a child the same shall be recorded under sub-section (2) in a simple language so that the child understands contents being recorded.

(4) In case contents, are being recorded in the language not understood by the child or wherever it is deemed necessary, a translator or an interpreter, having such qualifications, experience and on payment of such fees as may be prescribed, shall be provided to the child if he fails to understand the same.

(5) Where the Special Juvenile Police Unit or local police is satisfied that the child against whom an offence has been committed is in need of care and protection, then, it shall, after recording the reasons in writing, make immediate arrangement to give him such care and protection (including admitting the child into shelter home or to the nearest hospital) within twenty-four hours of the report, as may be prescribed.

(6) The Special Juvenile Police Unit or local police shall, without unnecessary delay but within a period of twenty-four hours, report the matter to the Child Welfare Committee and the Special Court or where no Special Court has been designated, to the Court of Session, including need of the child for care and protection and steps taken in this regard.

(7) N o person shall incur any liability, whether civil or criminal, for giving the information in good faith for the purpose of sub-section (1).

Section 20 - Obligation of media, studio and photographic facilities to report cases

Any personnel of the media or hotel or lodge or hospital or club or studio or photographic facilities, by whatever name called, irrespective of the number of persons employed therein, shall, on coming across any material or object which is sexually exploitative of the child (including pornographic, sexually-related or making obscene representation of a child or children) through the use of any medium, shall provide such information to the Special Juvenile Police Unit, or to the local police, as the case may be.

Section 21 - Punishment for failure to report or record a case

(1) Any person, who fails to report the commission of an offence under subsection (1) of section 19 or section 20 or who fails to record such offence under sub-section (2) of

section 19 shall be punished with imprisonment of either description which may extend to six months or with fine or with both.

(2) Any person, being in-charge of any company or an institution (by whatever name called) who fails to report the commission of an offence under sub-section (1) of section 19 in respect of a subordinate under his control, shall be punished with imprisonment for a term which may extend to one year and with fine.

(3) The provisions, of sub-section (7) shall not apply to a child under this Act.

Section 22 - Punishment for false complaint or false information

(1) Any person, who makes false complaint or provides false information against any person, in respect of an offence committed under sections 3, 5, 7 and section 9, solely with the intention to humiliate, extort or

threaten or defame him, shall be punished with imprisonment for a term which may extend to six months or with fine or with both.

(2) Where a false complaint has been made or false information has been provided by a child, no punishment shall be imposed on such child.

(3) Whoever, not being a child, makes a false complaint or provides false information against a child, knowing it to be false, thereby victimising such child in any of the offences under this Act, shall be punished with imprisonment which may extend to one year or with fine or with both.

Section 23 - Procedure for media

(1) No person shall make any report or present comments on any child from any form of media or studio or photographic facilities without having complete and authentic information, which may have the effect of lowering his reputation or infringing upon his privacy.

(2) No reports in any media shall disclose, the identity of a child including his name, address, photograph, family details, school, neighbourhood or any other particulars which may lead to disclosure of identity of the child:

Provided mat for reasons to be recorded in writing, the Special Court, competent to try the case under the Act, may permit such disclosure, if in its opinion such disclosure is in the interest of the child.

(3) The publisher or owner of the media or studio or photographic facilities shall be jointly and severally liable for the acts and omissions of his employee.

(4) Any person who contravenes the provisions of sub-section (1) or sub-section (2) shall be liable to be punished with imprisonment of either description for a period which shall not be less than six months but which may extend to one year or with fine or with both.

Section 24 - Recording of statement of a child

(1) The statement of the child shall be recorded at the residence of the child or at a place where he usually resides or at the place of his choice and as far as practicable by a woman police officer not below the rank of sub-inspector.

(2) The police officer while recording the statement of the child shall not be in uniform.

(3) The police officer making the investigation, shall, while examining the child, ensure that at no point of time the child come in the contact in any way with the accused.

(4) No child shall be detained in the police station in the night for any reason.

(5) The police officer shall ensure that the identity of the child is protected from the public media, unless otherwise directed by the Special Court in the interest of the child.

Section 25 - Recording of statement of a child by Magistrate

(1) If the statement of the child is being recorded under section 164 of the Code of Criminal Procedure, 1973(2 of 1974) (herein referred to as the Code), the Magistrate recording such statement shall, notwithstanding anything contained therein, record the statement as spoken by the child: Provided that the provisions contained in the first proviso to sub-section (1) of section 164 of the Code shall, so far it permits the presence of the advocate of the accused shall not apply in this case.

(2) The Magistrate shall provide to the child and his parents or his representative, a copy of the document specified under section 207 of the Code, upon the final report being filed by the police under section 173 of that Code.

Section 26 - Additional provisions regarding statement to be recorded

(1) The Magistrate or the police officer, as the case may be, shall record the statement as spoken by the child in the presence of the parents of the child or any other person in whom the child has trust or confidence.

(2) Wherever necessary, the Magistrate or the police officer, as the case may be, may take the assistance of a translator or an interpreter, having such qualifications, experience and on payment of such fees as may be prescribed, while recording the statement of the child.

(3) The Magistrate or the police officer, as the case may be, may, in the case of a child having a mental or physical disability, seek the assistance of a special educator or any person familiar with the manner of communication of

the child or an expert in that field, having such qualifications, experience and on payment of such fees as may be prescribed, to record the statement of the child.

(4) Wherever possible, the Magistrate or the police officer, as the case may be, shall ensure that the statement of the child is also recorded by audio-video electronic means.

Section 27 - Medical examination of a child

(1) The medical examination of a child in respect of whom any offence has been committed under this Act, shall, notwithstanding mat a First Information Report or complaint has not been registered for the offences under this Act, be conducted in accordance with section 164A of the Code of Criminal Procedure, 1973(2 of 1974).

(2) In case the victim is a girl child, the medical examination shall be conducted by a woman doctor.

(3) The medical examination shall be conducted in the presence of the parent of the child or any other person in whom the child reposes trust or confidence.

(4) Where, in case the parent of the child or other person referred to in sub-section

(3) cannot be present, for any reason, during the medical examination of the child, the medical examination shall be conducted in the presence of a woman nominated by the head of the medical institution.

Section 28 - Designation of Special Courts

(1) For the purposes of providing a speedy trial, the State Government shall in consultation with the Chief Justice of the High Court, by notification in the Official Gazette, designate for each district, a Court of Session to be a Special Court to try the offences under the Act:

Provided that if a Court of Session is notified as a children's court under the Commissions for Protection of Child Rights Act, 2005(4 of 2006) or a Special Court designated for similar purposes under any other law for the time being in force, then, such court shall be deemed to be a Special Court under this section.

(2) While trying an offence under this Act, a Special Court shall also try an offence [other than the offence referred to in sub-section (1)], with which the accused may, under the Code of Criminal Procedure, 1973(2 of 1974), be charged at the same trial.

(3) The Special Court constituted under this Act, notwithstanding anything in the Information Technology Act, 2000(21 of 2000), shall have jurisdiction to try offences under section 67B of that Act in so far as it relates to publication or transmission of sexually explicit material depicting children in any act, or conduct or manner or facilitates abuse of children online.

Section 29 - Presumption as to certain offences

Where a person is prosecuted for committing or abetting or attempting to commit any offence under sections 3, 5, 7 and section 9 of this Act, the Special Court shall presume, that such person has committed or abetted or attempted to commit the offence, as the case may be unless the contrary is proved.

Section 30 - Presumption of culpable mental state

(1) In any prosecution for any offence under this Act which requires a culpable mental state on the part of the accused, the Special Court shall presume the existence of such mental state but it shall be a defence for the accused to prove the fact that he had no such mental state with respect to the act charged as an offence in that prosecution.

(2) For the purposes of this section, a fact is said to be proved only when the Special Court believes it to exist beyond reasonable doubt and not merely when its existence is established by a preponderance of probability.

Explanation.—In this section, "culpable mental state" includes intention, motive, knowledge of a fact and the belief in, or reason to believe, a fact.

Section 31 - Application of Code of Criminal Procedure, 1973 to proceedings before a Special Court

Save as otherwise provided in this Act, the provisions of the Code of Criminal Procedure, 1973(2 of 1974) (including the provisions as to bail and bonds) shall apply to the

proceedings before a Special Court and for the purposes of the said provisions, the Special Court shall be deemed to be a Court of Sessions and the person conducting a prosecution before a Special Court, shall be deemed to be a Public Prosecutor.

Section 32 - Special Public Prosecutors

(1) The State Government shall, by notification in the Official Gazette, appoint a Special Public Prosecutor for every Special Court for conducting cases only under the provisions of this Act.

(2) A person shall be eligible to be appointed as a Special Public Prosecutor under sub-section (7) only if he had been in practice for not less than seven years as an advocate.

(3) Every person appointed as a Special Public Prosecutor under this section shall be deemed to be a Public Prosecutor within the meaning of clause (a) of section 2 of the Code of Criminal Procedure, 1973(2 of 1974) and provision of that Code shall have effect accordingly.

Section 33 - Procedure and powers of Special Court

(1) A Special Court may take cognizance of any offence, without the accused being committed to it for trial, upon receiving a complaint of facts which constitute such offence, or upon a police report of such facts.

(2) The Special Public Prosecutor, or as the case may be, the counsel appearing for the accused shall, while recording the examination-in-chief, cross-examination or re- examination of the child, communicate the questions to be put to the child to the Special Court which shall in turn put those questions to the child.

(3) The Special Court may, if it considers necessary, permit frequent breaks for the child during the trial.

(4) The Special Court shall create a child-friendly atmosphere by allowing a family member, a guardian, a friend or a relative, in whom the child has trust or confidence, to be present in the court.

(5) The Special Court shall ensure that the child is not called repeatedly to testify in the court.

(6) The Special Court shall not permit aggressive questioning or character assassination of the child and ensure that dignity of the child is maintained at all times during the trial.

(7) The Special Court shall ensure that the identity of the child is not disclosed at any time during the course of investigation or trial:

Provided that for reasons to be recorded in writing, the Special Court may permit such disclosure, if in its opinion such disclosure is in the interest of the child.

Explanation.—For the purposes of this sub-section, the identity of the child shall include the identity of the child's family, school, relatives, neighbourhood or any other information by which the identity of the child may be revealed.

(8) In appropriate cases, the Special Court may, in addition to the punishment, direct payment of such compensation as may be prescribed to the child for any physical or mental trauma caused to him or for immediate rehabilitation of such child.

(9) Subject to the provisions of this Act, a Special Court shall, for the purpose of the trial of any offence under this Act, have all the powers of a Court of Session and shall try such offence as if it were a Court of Session, and as far as may be, in accordance
with the procedure specified in the Code of Criminal Procedure, 1973(2 of 1974) for trial before a Court of Session.

Section 34 - Procedure in case of commission of offence by child and determination of age by Special Court

(1) Where any offence under this Act is committed by a child, such child shall be dealt with under the provisions of [17][the Juvenile Justice (Care and Protection of Children) Act, 2015 (2 of 2016)].

(2) If any question arises in any proceeding before the Special Court whether a person is a child or not, such question shall be determined by the Special Court after satisfying itself about the age of such person and it shall record in writing its reasons for such determination.

(3) No order made by the Special Court shall be deemed to be invalid merely by any subsequent proof that the age of a person as determined by it under sub-section (2) was not the correct age of that person.

1. Substituted by Protection Of Children From Sexual Offences (Amendment) Act, 2019, w.e.f. 16.08.2019 for the following:- "the Juvenile Justice (Care and Protection of Children) Act, 2000, (56 of 2000)"

17.

Section 35 - Period for recording of evidence of child and disposal of case

(1) The evidence of the child shall be recorded within a period of thirty days of the Special Court taking cognizance of the offence and reasons for delay, if any, shall be recorded by the Special Court.

(2) The Special Court shall complete the trial, as far as possible, within a period of one year from the date of taking cognizance of the offence.

Section 36 - Child not to see accused at the time of testifying

(1) The Special Court shall ensure that the child is not exposed in any way to the accused at the time of recording of the evidence, while at the same time ensuring that the accused is in a position to hear the statement of the child and communicate with his advocate.

(2) For the purposes of sub-section (1), the Special Court may record the statement of a child through video conferencing or by utilising single visibility mirrors or curtains or any other device.

Section 37 - Trials to be conducted in camera

The Special Court shall try cases in camera and in the presence of the parents of the child or any other person in whom the child has trust or confidence:

Provided that where the Special Court is of the opinion that the child needs to be examined at a place other than the court, it shall proceed to issue a commission in accordance with the provisions of section 284 of the Code of Criminal Procedure, 1973(2 of 1974).

CHAPTER

26

The Protection of Children from Sexual Offences Rules, 2020

1. **(1) Short title and commencement.**—These rules may be called the Protection of Children from Sexual Offences Rules, 2020.

   (2) They shall come into force on the date of their publication in the Official Gazette.

2. **Definitions.**—(1) In these rules, unless the context otherwise requires,–

(a) "Act" means the Protection of Children from Sexual Offences Act, 2012 (32 of 2012);

(b) "District Child Protection Unit" (DCPU) means the District Child Protection Unit established by the State Government under section 106 of the Juvenile Justice (Care and Protection of Children) Act, 2015 (2 of 2016);

(c) "expert" means a person trained in mental health, medicine, child development or other relevant discipline, who may be required to facilitate communication with a child whose ability to communicate has been affected by trauma, disability or any other vulnerability;

(d) "special educator" means a person trained in communication with children with disabilities in a way that addresses the child's individual abilities and needs, which include challenges with learning and communication, emotional and behavioral issues, physical disabilities, and developmental issues.

Explanation.—For the purposes of this clause, the expression "disabilities", shall carry the same meaning as defined in clause (s) of section 2 of the Rights of Persons with Disabilities Act, 2016 (49 of 2016);

(e) "Person familiar with the manner of communication of the child" means a parent or family member of a child or a member of child's shared household or any person in whom the child reposes trust and confidence, who is familiar with that child's unique manner of communication, and whose presence may be required for or be conducive to more effective communication with the child;

(f) "support person" means a person assigned by the Child Welfare Committee, in accordance with sub-rule (7) of rule 4, to render assistance to the child through the process of investigation and trial, or any other person assisting the child in the pre-trial or trial process in respect of an offence under the Act;

(2) Words and expressions used and not defined in these rules but defined in the Act shall have the meanings respectively assigned to them under the Act.

3. **Awareness generation and capacity building.**—(1) The Central Government, or as the case may be, the State Government shall prepare age-appropriate educational material and curriculum for children, informing them about various aspects of personal safety, including—

(i) measures to protect their physical, and virtual identity; and to safeguard their emotional and mental wellbeing;

(ii) prevention and protection from sexual offences;

(iii) reporting mechanisms, including Child helpline-1098 services;

(iv) inculcating gender sensitivity, gender equality and gender equity for effective prevention of offences under the Act.

(2) Suitable material and information may be disseminated by the respective Governments in all public places such as panchayatbhavans, community centers, schools and colleges, bus terminals, railway stations, places of congregation, airports, taxi stands, cinema halls and such other prominent places and also be disseminated in suitable form in virtual spaces such as internet and social media.

(3) The Central Government and every State Government shall take all suitable measures to spread awareness about possible risks and vulnerabilities, signs of abuse, information about rights of children under the Act along with access to support and services available for children.

(4) Any institution housing children or coming in regular contact with children including schools, creches, sports academies or any other facility for children must ensure a police verification and background check on periodic basis, of every staff, teaching or non-teaching, regular or contractual, or any other person being an employee of such Institution coming in contact with the child. Such Institution shall also ensure that

periodic training is organised for sensitising them on child safety and protection.

(5) The respective Governments shall formulate a child protection policy based on the principle of zero-tolerance to violence against children, which shall be adopted by all institutions, organizations, or any other agency working with, or coming in contact with children.

(6) The Central Government and every State Government shall provide periodic trainings including orientation programmes, sensitization workshops and refresher courses to all persons, whether regular or contractual, coming in contact with the children, to sensitize them about child safety and protection and educate them regarding their responsibility under the Act. Orientation programme and intensive courses may also be organized for police personnel and forensic experts for building their capacities in their respective roles on a regular basis.

4. **Procedure regarding care and protection of child.**— (1) Where any Special Juvenile Police Unit (hereafter referred to as "SJPU") or the local police receives any information under sub-section (1) of section19 of the Act from any person including the child, the SJPU or local police receiving the report of such information shall forthwith disclose to the person making the report, the following details:-

(i) his or her name and designation;

(ii) the address and telephone number;

(iii) the name, designation and contact details of the officer who supervises the officer receiving the information.

(2) If any such information regarding the commission of an offence under the provisions of the Act is received by the child helpline-1098, the child helpline shall immediately report such information to SJPU or Local Police.

(3) Where an SJPU or the local police, as the case may be, receives information in accordance with the provisions contained under sub-section (1) of section 19 of the Act in respect of an offence that has been committed or attempted or is likely to be committed, the authority concerned shall, where applicable, —

(a) proceed to record and register a First Information Report as per the provisions of section154 of the Code of Criminal Procedure, 1973 (2 of 1974), and furnish a copy thereof free of cost to the person making such report, as per sub-section (2) of section154 of that Code;

(b) where the child needs emergency medical care as described under sub-section (5) of section 19 of the Act or under these rules, arrange for the child to access such care, in accordance with rule 6;

(c) take the child to the hospital for the medical examination in accordance with section 27 of the Act;

(d) ensure that the samples collected for the purposes of the forensic tests are sent to the forensic laboratory immediately;

(e) inform the child and child's parent or guardian or other person in whom the child has trust and confidence of the availability of support services including counselling, and assist them in contacting the persons who are responsible for providing these services and relief;

(f) inform the child and child's parent or guardian or other person in whom the child has trust and confidence as to the right of the child to legal advice and counsel and the right to be represented by a lawyer, in accordance with section 40 of the Act.

(4) Where the SJPU or the local police receives information under sub-section (1) of section 19 of the Act, and has a reasonable apprehension that the offence has been committed or attempted or is likely to be committed by a person living in the same or shared household with the child, or the child is living in a child care institution and is without parental support, or the child is found to be without any home and parental support, the concerned SJPU, or the local police shall produce the child before the concerned Child Welfare Committee (hereafter referred to as "CWC") within 24 hours of receipt of such report, together with reasons in writing as to whether the child is in need of care and protection under sub-section (5) of section 19 of the Act, and with a request for a detailed assessment by the CWC.

(5) Upon receipt of a report under sub-rule (3), the concerned CWC must proceed, in accordance with its powers under sub-section (1) of section 31 of the Juvenile Justice Act, 2015 (2 of 2016), to make a determination within three days, either on its own or with the assistance of a social

worker, as to whether the child needs to be taken out of the custody of child's family or shared household and placed in a children's home or a shelter home.

(6) In making determination under sub-rule (4), the CWC shall take into account any preference or opinion expressed by the child on the matter, together with the best interests of the child, having regard to the following considerations, namely:—

(i) the capacity of the parents, or of either parent, or of any other person in whom the child has trust and confidence, to provide for the immediate care and protection needs of the child, including medical needs and counseling;

(ii) the need for the child to remain in the care of parent's, family and extended family and to maintain a connection with them;

(iii) the child's age and level of maturity, gender, and social and economic background;

(iv) disability of the child, if any;

(v) any chronic illness from which a child may suffer;

(vi) any history of family violence involving the child or a family member of the child; and,

(vii) any other relevant factors that may have a bearing on the best interests of the child:

Provided that prior to making such determination, an inquiry shall be conducted in such a way that the child is not unnecessarily exposed to injury or inconvenience.

(7) The child and child's parent or guardian or any other person in whom the child has trust and confidence and with whom the child has been living, who is affected by such determination, shall be informed that such determination is being considered.

(8) The CWC, on receiving a report under sub-section (6) of section 19 of the Act or on the basis of its assessment made under sub-rule (5), and with the consent of the child and child's parent or guardian or other person in whom the child has trust and confidence, may provide a support person to render assistance to the child in all possible manner throughout the

process of investigation and trial, and shall immediately inform the SJPU or Local Police about providing a support person to the child.

(9) The support person shall at all times maintain the confidentiality of all information pertaining to the child to which he or she has access and shall keep the child and child's parent or guardian or other person in whom the child has trust and confidence, informed regarding the proceedings of the case, including available assistance, judicial procedures, and potential outcomes. The Support person shall also inform the child of the role the Support person may play in the judicial process and ensure that any concerns that the child may have, regarding child's safety in relation to the accused and the manner in which the Support person would like to provide child's testimony, are conveyed to the relevant authorities.

(10) Where a support person has been provided to the child, the SJPU or the local police shall, within 24 hours of making such assignment, inform the Special Court in writing.

(11) The services of the support person may be terminated by the CWC upon request by the child and child's parent or guardian or person in whom the child has trust and confidence, and the child requesting the termination shall not be required to assign any reason for such request. The Special Court shall be given in writing such information.

(12) The CWC shall also Seek monthly reports from support person till the completion of trial, with respect to condition and care of child, including the family situation focusing on the physical, emotional and mental wellbeing, and progress towards healing from trauma; engage with medical care facilities, in coordination with the support person, to ensure need-based continued medical support to the child, including psychological care and counseling; and shall ensure resumption of education of the child, or continued education of the child, or shifting of the child to a new school, if required.

(13) It shall be the responsibility of the SJPU, or the local police to keep the child and child's parent or guardian or other person in whom the child has trust and confidence, and where a support person has been assigned,

such person, informed about the developments, including the arrest of the accused, applications filed and other court proceedings.

(14) SJPU or the local police shall also inform the child and child's parents or guardian or other person in whom the child has trust and confidence about their entitlements and services available to them under the Act or any other law for the time being applicable as per **Form-A.** It shall also complete the Preliminary Assessment Report in **Form B** within 24 hours of the registration of the First Information Report and submit it to the CWC.

(15) The information to be provided by the SJPU, local police, or support person, to the child and child's parents or guardian or other person in whom the child has trust and confidence, includes but is not limited to the following:-

(i) the availability of public and private emergency and crisis services;
(ii) the procedural steps involved in a criminal prosecution;
(iii) the availability of victim's compensation benefits;
(iv) the status of the investigation of the crime, to the extent it is appropriate to inform the victim and to the extent that it will not interfere with the investigation;
(v) the arrest of a suspected offender;
(vi) the filing of charges against a suspected offender;
(vii) the schedule of court proceedings that the child is either required to attend or is entitled to attend;
(viii) the bail, release or detention status of an offender or suspected offender;
(ix) the rendering of a verdict after trial; and
(x) the sentence imposed on an offender.

5. **Interpreters, translators, special educators, experts and support persons.**—(1) In each district, the DCPU shall maintain a register with names, addresses and other contact details of interpreters, translators, experts, special educators and support persons for the purposes of the Act, and this register shall be made available to the SJPU, local police, magistrate or Special Court, as and when required.

(2) The qualifications and experience of the interpreters, translators, special educators, experts and support persons engaged for the purposes of sub-section (4) of section 19, sub-sections (3) and (4) of section 26 and section 38 of the Act,and rule 4 respectively shall be as indicated in these rules.

(3) Where an interpreter, translator, or special educator is engaged, otherwise than from the list maintained by the DCPU under sub-rule (1), the requirements prescribed under sub-rules (4) and (5) of this rule may be relaxed on evidence of relevant experience or formal education or training or demonstrated proof of fluency in the relevant languages by the interpreter, translator, or special educator, subject to the satisfaction of the DCPU, Special Court or other authority concerned.

(4) Interpreters and translators engaged under sub-rule (1) should have functional familiarity with language spoken by the child as well as the official language of the state, either by virtue of such language being child's mother tongue or medium of instruction at school at least up to primary school level, or by the interpreter or translator having acquired knowledge of such language through child's vocation, profession, or residence in the area where that language is spoken.

(5) Sign language interpreters, special educators and experts entered in the register under sub-rule(1) should have relevant qualifications in sign language or special education, or in the case of an expert, in the relevant discipline, from a recognised University or an institution recognised by the Rehabilitation Council of India.

(6) Support person may be a person or organisation working in the field of child rights or child protection, or an official of a children's home or shelter home having custody of the child, or a person employed by the DCPU:

Provided that nothing in these rules shall prevent the child and child's parents or guardian or other person in whom the child has trust and confidence from seeking the assistance of any person or organisation for proceedings under the Act.

(7) Payment for the services of an interpreter, translator, special educator, expert or support person whose name is enrolled in the register maintained

under sub-rule (1) or otherwise, shall be made by the State Government from the Fund maintained under section 105 of the Juvenile Justice Act, 2015 (2 of 2016), or from other funds placed at the disposal of the DCPU.

(8) Any interpreter, translator, special educator, expert or support person engaged for the purpose of assisting a child under this Act, shall be paid a fee which shall be prescribed by the State Government, but which, shall not be less than the amount prescribed for a skilled worker under the Minimum Wages Act, 1948 (11 of 1948).

(9) Any preference expressed by the child at any stage after information is received under sub-section(1) of section 19 of the Act, as to the gender of the interpreter, translator, special educator, expert or support person, may be taken into consideration, and where necessary, more than one such person may be engaged in order to facilitate communication with the child.

(10) The interpreter, translator, special educator, expert, support person or person familiar with the manner of communication of the child engaged to provide services for the purposes of the Act shall be unbiased and impartial and shall disclose any real or perceived conflict of interest and shall render a complete and accurate interpretation or translation without any additions or omissions, in accordance with section 282 of the Code of Criminal Procedure, 1973 (2 of 1974).

(11) In proceedings under section 38, the Special Court shall ascertain whether the child speaks the language of the court adequately, and that the engagement of any interpreter, translator, special educator, expert, support person or other person familiar with the manner of communication of the child, who has been engaged to facilitate communication with the child, does not involve any conflict of interest.

(12) Any interpreter, translator, special educator, expert or support person appointed under the Act shall be bound by the rules of confidentiality, as described under section 127 read with section 126 of the Indian Evidence Act, 1872 (1 of 1872).

6. **Medical aid and care.**—(1) Where an officer of the SJPU, or the local police receives information under section 19 of the Act that an offence under the Act has been committed, and is satisfied that the child against whom an offence has been committed is in need of urgent medical care and protection, such officer, or as the case may be, the local police shall, within 24 hours of receiving such information, arrange to take such child to the nearest hospital or medical care facility center for emergency medical care:

   Provided that where an offence has been committed under sections 3, 5, 7 or 9 of the Act, the victim shall be referred to emergency medical care.

(2) Emergency medical care shall be rendered in such a manner as to protect the privacy of the child, and in the presence of the parent or guardian or any other person in whom the child has trust and confidence.

(3) No medical practitioner, hospital or other medical facility center rendering emergency medical care to a child shall demand any legal or magisterial requisition or other documentation as a pre-requisite to rendering such care.

(4) The registered medical practitioner rendering medical care shall attend to the needs of the child, including:

(a) treatment for cuts, bruises, and other injuries including genital injuries, if any;

(b) treatment for exposure to sexually transmitted diseases (STDs) including prophylaxis for identified STDs;

(c) treatment for exposure to Human Immunodeficiency Virus (HIV), including prophylaxis for HIV after necessary consultation with infectious disease experts;

(d) possible pregnancy and emergency contraceptives should be discussed with the pubertal child and her parent or any other person in whom the child has trust and confidence; and,

(e) wherever necessary, a referral or consultation for mental or psychological health needs, or other counseling, or drug de-addiction services and programmes should be made.

(5) The registered medical practitioner shall submit the report on the condition of the child within 24 hrs to the SJPU or Local Police.

(6) Any forensic evidence collected in the course of rendering emergency medical care must be collected in accordance with section 27 of the Act.

(7) If the child is found to be pregnant, then the registered medical practitioner shall counsel the child, and her parents or guardians, or support person, regarding the various lawful options available to the child as per the Medical Termination of Pregnancy Act 1971 and the Juvenile Justice (Care and Protection of Children) Act 2015 (2 of 2016).

(8) If the child is found to have been administered any drugs or other intoxicating substances, access to drug de- addiction programme shall be ensured.

(9) If the Child is a divyang (person with disability), suitable measure and care shall be taken as per the provisions of The Rights of Persons with Disabilities Act, 2016 (49 of 2016).

7. **Legal aid and assistance.**—(1) The CWC shall make a recommendation to District Legal Services Authority (hereafter referred to as "DLSA") for legal aid and assistance.

(2) The legal aid and assistance shall be provided to the child in accordance with the provisions of the *Legal Services Authorities Act,* 1987 (39 of 1987).

8. **Special relief.**—(1) For special relief, if any, to be provided for contingencies such as food, clothes, transport and other essential needs, CWC may recommend immediate payment of such amount as it may assess to be required at that stage, to any of the following:-

(i) the DLSA under Section 357A; or;
(ii) the DCPU out of such funds placed at their disposal by state or;
(iii) funds maintained under section105 of the Juvenile Justice (Care and Protection of Children) Act,2015 (2 of 2016);

(2) Such immediate payment shall be made within a week of receipt of recommendation from the CWC.

9. **Compensation.**—(1) The Special Court may, in appropriate cases, on its own or on an application filed by or on behalf of the child, pass an order for interim compensation to meet the needs of the child for relief or rehabilitation at any stage after registration of the First Information Report. Such interim compensation paid to the child shall be adjusted against the final compensation, if any.

(2) The Special Court may, on its own or on an application filed by or on behalf of the victim, recommend the award of compensation where the accused is convicted, or where the case ends in acquittal or discharge, or the accused is not traced or identified, and in the opinion of the Special Court the child has suffered loss or injury as a result of that offence.

(3) Where the Special Court, under sub-section (8) of section 33 of the Act read with sub-sections (2) and (3) of section 357A of the Code of Criminal Procedure, 1973 (2 of 1974) makes a direction for the award of compensation to the victim, it shall take into account all relevant factors relating to the loss or injury caused to the victim, including the following:-

(i) type of abuse, gravity of the offence and the severity of the mental or physical harm or injury suffered by the child;

(ii) the expenditure incurred or likely to be incurred on child's medical treatment for physical or mental health or on both;

(iii) loss of educational opportunity as a consequence of the offence, including absence from school due to mental trauma, bodily injury, medical treatment, investigation and trial of the offence, or any other reason;

(iv) loss of employment as a result of the offence, including absence from place of employment due to mental trauma, bodily injury, medical treatment, investigation and trial of the offence, or any other reason;

(v) the relationship of the child to the offender, if any;

(vi) whether the abuse was a single isolated incidence or whether the abuse took place over a period of time;

(vii) whether the child became pregnant as a result of the offence;

(viii) whether the child contracted a sexually transmitted disease (STD) as a result of the offence;

(ix) whether the child contracted human immunodeficiency virus (HIV) as a result of the offence;

(x) any disability suffered by the child as a result of the offence;

(xi) financial condition of the child against whom the offence has been committed so as to determine such child's need for rehabilitation;

(xii) any other factor that the Special Court may consider to be relevant.

(4) The compensation awarded by the Special Court is to be paid by the State Government from the Victims Compensation Fund or other scheme or fund established by it for the purposes of compensating and rehabilitating victims under section 357A of the Code of Criminal Procedure, 1973 or any other law for the time being in force, or, where such fund or scheme does not exist, by the State Government.

(5) The State Government shall pay the compensation ordered by the Special Court within 30 days of receipt of such order.

(6) Nothing in these rules shall prevent a child or child's parent or guardian or any other person in whom the child has trust and confidence from submitting an application for seeking relief under any other rules or scheme of the Central Government or State Government.

10. **Procedure for imposition of fine and payment thereof.**—(1) The CWC shall coordinate with the DLSA to ensure that any amount of fine imposed by the Special Court under the Act which is to be paid to the victim, is in fact paid to the child.

(2) The CWC will also facilitate any procedure for opening a bank account, arranging for identity proofs, etc., with the assistance of DCPU and support person.

11. **Reporting of pornographic material involving a child.**—(1)Any person who has received any pornographic material involving a child or any information regarding such pornographic material being stored, possessed, distributed, circulated, transmitted, facilitated, propagated or displayed, or is likely to be distributed, facilitated or transmitted in any manner shall report the contents to the SJPU or local police, or as the case may be, cyber-crime portal (cybercrime.gov.in) and upon such receipt of the

report, the SJPU or local police or the cyber-crime portal take necessary action as per the directions of the Government issued from time to time.

(2) In case the "person" as mentioned in sub-rule (1) is an "intermediary" as defined in clause (w) of sub-section (1) of section 2 of the Information Technology Act,2000, such person shall in addition to reporting, as provided under sub-rule(1), also hand over the necessary material including the source from which such material may have originated to the SJPU or local police, or as the case may be, cyber-crime portal (cybercrime.gov.in) and upon such receipt of the said material, the SJPU or local police or the cyber-crime portal take necessary action as per the directions of the Government issued from time to time.

(3) The report shall include the details of the device in which such pornographic content was noticed and the suspected device from which such content was received including the platform on which the content was displayed.

(4) The Central Government and every State Government shall make all endeavors to create widespread awareness about the procedures of making such reports from time to time.

12. **Monitoring of implementation of the Act.**—(1) The National Commission for the Protection of Child Rights (hereafter referred to as "NCPCR") or the State Commission for the Protection of Child Rights (hereafter referred to as "SCPCR"), as the case may be, shall in addition to the functions assigned to them under the Commissions for Protection of Child Rights Act, 2005 (4 of 2006), perform the following functions for implementation of the provisions of the Act—

(a) monitor the designation of Special Courts by State Governments;

(b) monitor the appointment of the Special Public Prosecutors by the State Governments;

(c) monitor the formulation of the guidelines described in section 39 of the Act by the State Governments, for the use of non-governmental organisations, professionals and experts or persons having knowledge of psychology, social work, physical health, mental health and child development to be associated with the pre-trial and trial stage to assist the child, and to monitor the application of these guidelines;

(d) monitor the designing and implementation of modules for training police personnel and other concerned persons, including officers of the Centre and State Governments, for the effective discharge of their functions under the Act;

(e) monitor and support the Central Government and State Governments for the dissemination of information relating to the provisions of the Act through media including the television, radio and print media at regular intervals, so as to make the general public, children as well as their parents and guardians aware of the provisions of the Act.

(f) call for a report on any specific case of child sexual abuse falling within the jurisdiction of a CWC.

(g) collect information and data on its own or from the relevant agencies regarding reported cases of sexual abuse and their disposal under the processes provided under the Act, including information on the following:-

(i) number and details of offences reported under the Act;

(ii) whether the procedures prescribed under the Act and rules were followed, including those regarding timeframes;

(iii) details of arrangements for care and protection of victims of offences under this Act, including arrangements for emergency medical care and medical examination; and,

(iv) details regarding assessment of the need for care and protection of a child by the concerned CWC in any specific case;

(h) use the information so collected to assess the implementation of the provisions of the Act. The report on monitoring of the Act shall be included in a separate chapter in the annual report of the NCPCR or the SCPCR.

(2) The concerned authorities mandated to collect data, under the Act, shall share such data with the Central Government and every State Government, NCPCR and SCPCRs.

13. **Repeal.**—The Protection of Children from Sexual Offences Rules, 2012 are hereby repealed, except as respects things done or omitted to be done before such repeal.

FORM -A

Entitlement of children who have suffered sexual abuse to receive information and services

1. To receive a copy of the FIR.
2. To receive adequate security and protection by Police.
3. To receive immediate and free medical examination by civil hospital/ PHC etc.
4. To receive Counseling and consultation for mental and psychological well being
5. For Recording of statement of child by woman police officer at child's home or any other place convenient to child
6. To be moved to a Child Care Institution where offence was at home or in a shared household, to the custody of a person whom child reposes faith.
7. For Immediate aid and assistance on the recommendation of CWC.
8. For being kept away from accused at all times, during trial and otherwise.
9. To have an interpreter or translator, where needed.
10. To have special educator for the child or other specialized person where child is disabled.
11. For Free Legal Aid.
12. For Support Person to be appointed by Child Welfare Committee.
13. To continue with education.
14. To privacy and confidentiality.
15. For list of Important Contact No.'s including that of the District Magistrate and the Superintendent of Police.

Duty Officer

Date: **(Name & Designation to be mentioned)**

I have received a copy of 'Form-A'
(Signature of Victim/Parent/Guardian)

(Note :The form may be converted in local and simple Child friendly language)

PRELIMINARY ASSESSMENT REPORT

FORM-B

PARAMETERS	COMMENT
1. Age of the victim	
2. Relationship of child to the offender	
3. Type of abuse and gravity of the offence	
4. Available details and severity of mental and physical harm/injury suffered by the child	
5. Whether the child is disabled (physical, mental or intellectual)	
6. Details regarding economic status of victim's parents, total number of child's family members, occupation of child's parents and monthly family income.	
7. Whether the victim has undergone or is undergoing any medical treatment due to incident of the present case or needs medical treatment on account of offence.	
8. Whether there has been loss of educational opportunity as a consequence of the offence, including absence from school due to mental trauma, bodily injury, medical treatment, investigation and trial or other reason?	
9. Whether the abuse was a single isolated incident or whether the abuse took place over a period of time?	
10. Whether the parents of victim are undergoing any treatment or have any health issues?	
11. Aadhar No. of the child, if available.	

Date: Station House Officer

www.ingramcontent.com/pod-product-compliance
Lightning Source LLC
LaVergne TN
LVHW091318150826
845673LV00006B/1690

9798894460925